Library
Research Guide
to
History

"Library Research Guides" Series

JAMES R. KENNEDY, JR. and
THOMAS G. KIRK, JR., Editors

Library Research Guide to History

Illustrated Search Strategy and Sources

by
ELIZABETH FRICK
Head of User Services
University of Colorado Library,
Colorado Springs

("Library Research Guides" Series, No. 4)

Pierian Press
ANN ARBOR, MICHIGAN

International Standard Book Numbers: 0-87650-119-6 (cloth);
0-87650-123-4 (paper)
Library of Congress Catalog Card Number: 80-83514

Pierian Press, P.O. Box 1808, Ann Arbor, Michigan 48106
Printed in the United States of America

Note: Dashes appear as double
hyphens throughout the text.

Contents

The researcher must again and again *imagine* the kind of source he would like to have before he can find it . . . . By that ingenious balancing of wish and reason which is true imagination, the seeker can make his way from what he knows and possesses to what he must possess in order to know more.

There is in any piece of research so much to be read, noted down, compared, verified, indexed, grouped, organized, and recopied, that unless one is capable of adhering to a system the chances of error grow alarming, while the task itself turns into a perpetual panicky emergency . . . .

—Reprinted by permission of
Harcourt Brace Jovanovich, Inc.
from *THE MODERN RESEARCHER*, 3d ed., ©1977,
by Jacques Barzun and Henry F. Graff.

Is This the Book You Need?

The answer is yes if you find yourself in one of the following situations:

1. If you are a *college junior or senior majoring in history*, you will need to know how to locate appropriate library materials for term papers. This book assumes the card catalog and the *Readers' Guide* are "old friends," but you need to be introduced to the basic reference sources for history. If, by some chance, you do *not* know how to use the card catalog and the *Readers' Guide* well, or have not written term papers for other courses that provided good library experience, then read the warning in the last two paragraphs of this preface.

2. If you are a *graduate student in history*, you will be writing a number of research papers. This book will guide you to many useful reference sources.

3. If you are a *professor of history* or a *reference librarian*, students often ask you for advice on how to find library materials for term papers in history. It would be good to be able to recommend a library guide to these students. This is it.

Caveat Lector (Let the Reader Beware)

Do not begin with this book:

1. If you have somehow escaped learning how to use the card catalog and the *Readers' Guide*. Take the five-minute, self-graded test in Appendix II, in case you wonder how much you know. If you fail the test, save this book until you have read the pages on the card catalog and the *Readers' Guide* in such books as: Margaret G. Cook, *The New Library Key*, 3rd ed. (New York: Wilson, 1975); or Ella V. Aldrich, *Using Books and Libraries*, 5th ed. (Englewood Cliffs, NJ: Prentice-Hall, 1967).

2. If you need to know the general procedures for writing term papers, including notetaking, outlining, and bibliographical forms. Use this book in conjunction with: Kate L. Turabian, *Students' Guide for Writing College Papers*, 3rd ed. (Chicago: University of Chicago Press, 1976); or Porter G. Perrin, *Writer's Guide and Index to English*, 5th ed. (Glenview, IL: Scott, Foresman, 1972).

Acknowledgments

The thanks that I send to the following people for their support are only exceeded by the extent of their aid: Jim Kennedy, the editor with Tom Kirk, for the time and care that were put into the project; Evan Farber for all he has taught me as a librarian and as a person; the librarians at the University of Toronto for the beauty of their collection; Earlham College for the Faculty Development Grant that helped me get the project under way; Michael Herbison for his unfailing support (which included cheerful reminders of what critics could do to me); Theresa Sentman and Hope Farber for the meticulous quality of their typing; and three chickens, Kristin, Rachel, and Robin for their love. Finally, I want to express my warm love and affection for Stephen, and my continuing love and gratitude to Wilfrid and Elizabeth Sanders.

Had any one of these ingredients been missing, the project would have faltered. My heartfelt thanks to them and to all the others who have helped me.

Credits for Figures

Thanks are also due to the many publishers cited below who gave their permission to use excerpts from copyrighted works. Without their generosity this book could not have been the illustrated guide that was intended. Uncopyrighted materials are also cited below in order to make the list of figures complete.

Figure 1: *Encyclopedia Americana*. International edition. New York: Americana Corp., 1972, vol. 30, p.889; vol. 29, pp. 103, 104, 107.

Figure 2: Reprinted by permission of Charles Scribner's Sons from the *Dictionary of American History*, revised edition, volume 7, pp. 314, 315. Reprinted by permission of Charles Scribner's Sons from the *Dictionary of American History*, revised edition, volume 8, p. 494. Copyright (c) 1978 Charles Scribner's Sons.

Figure 3: A card showing how to note an item of bibliography.

Figure 4: *Encyclopedia Americana*. International edition. New York: Americana Corp., 1976, vol. 29, p. 103.

Figure 5: This material is reprinted from *Women and Society: A Critical Review of the Literature with a Selected Annotated Bibliography*, Marie Barovic Rosenberg and Len V. Bergstrom, editors (c) 1975, pp. Table of Contents, 124, 125 by permission of the publisher, Sage Publications, (Beverly Hills/London).

Figure 6: Krichmar, Albert. *The Women's Rights Movement in the United States, 1848-1970*. Metuchen, NJ: Scarecrow, 1972, p. 99.

Figure 7: Jacobs, Sue-Ellen. *Women in Perspective; A Guide for Cross-Cultural Studies*. Urbana, IL: University of Illinois Press, 1974, p. 205.

Figure 8: Sheehy, Eugene P. *Guide to Reference Books*. 9th ed. Chicago: American Library Association, 1976, pp. 611, 612. Reprinted by permission of the American Library Association, copyright (c) 1973 by the American Library Association.

Figure 9: De Santis, Vincent P. *The Gilded Age, 1877-1896*. Northbrook, IL: AHM, 1973, pp. 89, 90.

Figure 10: *Bibliographic Index . . . 1972*. New York: H.W. Wilson, 1972, 1973, p. 454. Reproduced by permission of The H.W. Wilson Company.

Figure 11: *Harvard Guide to American History*, ed. by Frank Freidel. Rev. ed. Cambridge, MA: Belknap Press of Harvard University Press, 1974, vol. 1, pp. xii, 444, 445; vol. 2, p. 1290.

Figure 12: Tobias, Sheila, "The Study of Women," *Choice*, vol. 8, no. 10 (December, 1971), p. 1296.

Figure 13: *Supplement to LC Subject Headings, 1974--1976*. Washington, DC: Library of Congress, 1977, pp. 750--751.

Figure 14: Library of Congress catalog cards.

Figure 15: *Essay and General Literature Index, 1960-1964*. New York: H.W. Wilson, 1965, pp. 111, 1503, 1588. Reproduced by permission of the H.W. Wilson Company. Library of Congress catalog card.

Figure 16: *Book Review Digest* (1960). New York: H.W. Wilson, 1961, pp. 464, 465. Reproduced by permission of The H.W. Wilson Company.

Figure 17: *Book Review Index, 1971 Cumulation*. Detroit: Gale Research, 1974, p. 160.

Figure 18: *An Index to Book Reviews in the Humanities*. Detroit: Phillip Thomson, 1960, vol. 1, pp. 101, vi.

Figure 19: *Humanities Index*. New York: H.W. Wilson, 1976, vol. 2, p. 917. Reproduced by permission of The H.W. Wilson Company.

Figure 20: Scott, Anne Firor. Review of Ross Evans Paulson, *Women's Suffrage and Prohibition; A*

Anybody can make history.
Only a great man can write it.
Oscar Wilde, *Aphorisms*

Starting to Choose a Topic

Choosing a topic that interests you is a first key to a successful paper. Choosing an "easy" topic, or one that seems to be the professor's pet, will only result in a boring stretch of research. The enthusiasm you can generate for a topic that captures your interest will be reflected in your paper.

In choosing a topic for a paper in American history, perhaps your interest was first aroused by seeing a picture in a book of the frail Emmeline Pankhurst being carried off to prison by four stout gentlemen. Did you wonder then at the vehemence of the arrest? Perhaps you asked if American law had a similar reaction to suffragists. Or maybe, as you yourself voted in an election, you marvelled, as you felt the insignificance of your vote, that anyone would get excited enough to suffer force-feeding for the simple right to vote. Even current controversies over the Equal Rights Amendment and the opposition to it could have stirred your interest in historical precedents for opposition to such moves. Who on either side cares enough to put all that effort into the cause? Maybe the rich stuff of nineteenth century reform periodicals caught your eye. Who, you ask, were these indignant ladies who began by fighting for temperance and ended fighting for the right to vote, to have a say in their own governance? And what brave souls tried to withstand their impassioned logic?

It could simply be that your professor has given you a list of topics from which you may choose a theme, and the one which conjures up the liveliest associations is "Women's Suffrage in the United States." However you have arrived at the broad topic, hopefully you have found one that captures your imagination. It remains now to find the facts.

In the beginning a broad summary would be helpful in outlining the history of the subject. The subject will also need to be narrowed considerably, but we can discuss that problem later, in Chapter 2.

Looking for an Authoritative Summary of Your Topic

Right now you need that authoritative summary. Why? A summary is a good way to get a lot of information in as brief a manner as possible. Obviously. It is also an excellent way to divide a broad topic into manageable portions. For instance the women's suffrage movement could be viewed from several perspectives: you could divide it up chronologically into early beginnings, the long fight, success, and subsequent events, or you might choose to study its origins, the people involved in the long debate, the relationship of the suffrage movement to other contemporary events (e.g. the Civil War), or the history of the legislation that resulted.

A careful reading of a summary can also net you important information for later use. For example you will find the names of the most important leaders, names you can later use in locating biographical information in the *Dictionary of American Biography* (the major source of scholarly biography on deceased Americans); or dates which will give you a clue about where to start searching in indexes like *Poole's* or the *Readers' Guide* which cover periodicals of the time.

A summarizing article can also provide you with a balanced view and a bibliography. If an issue is controversial, a balanced summary will outline the various positions for you, as well as give you the names of their proponents. An immediate satisfaction can be the bibliography of major works on your topic that you may hope to find at the end of the summary. For such blessings it is worth looking for an authoritative summary.

Where can you find such summaries? Encyclopedias are the most obvious place to look, but there are also authoritative and concise summaries in some textbooks, in library books on reserve for the course and in other books the reference librarian can help you find. It remains true however that authoritative summaries are what good encyclopedias are all about. An encyclopedia article signed by a scholar in the field offers not only a clear outline and summation of the topic, but perhaps a new insight into the subject and surely a bibliography of the best standard books and articles on the topic.

There are two kinds of encyclopedias you should be aware of: first is the general encyclopedia covering as much of the world of knowledge as possible. Second there are the specialized encyclopedias which stay in one field and cover it in greater depth than is possible in a general encyclopedia.

An example of the general encyclopedia is the *Encyclopedia Americana*, 30 vols. (New York: Americana Corp., 1972). Your first approach in such a multi-volume work is best made via the index and here the search words you use will be important. For instance, notice in FIGURE 1 that there is nothing listed under the subject "Women's Suffrage," but under the broader "Women's Rights" you are referred to "Women, Legal Rights of" and the rather odd-sounding "Woman Suffrage." The last one, despite its oddity, appears to be most clearly on your topic.

When you look up "Woman Suffrage" in the index you

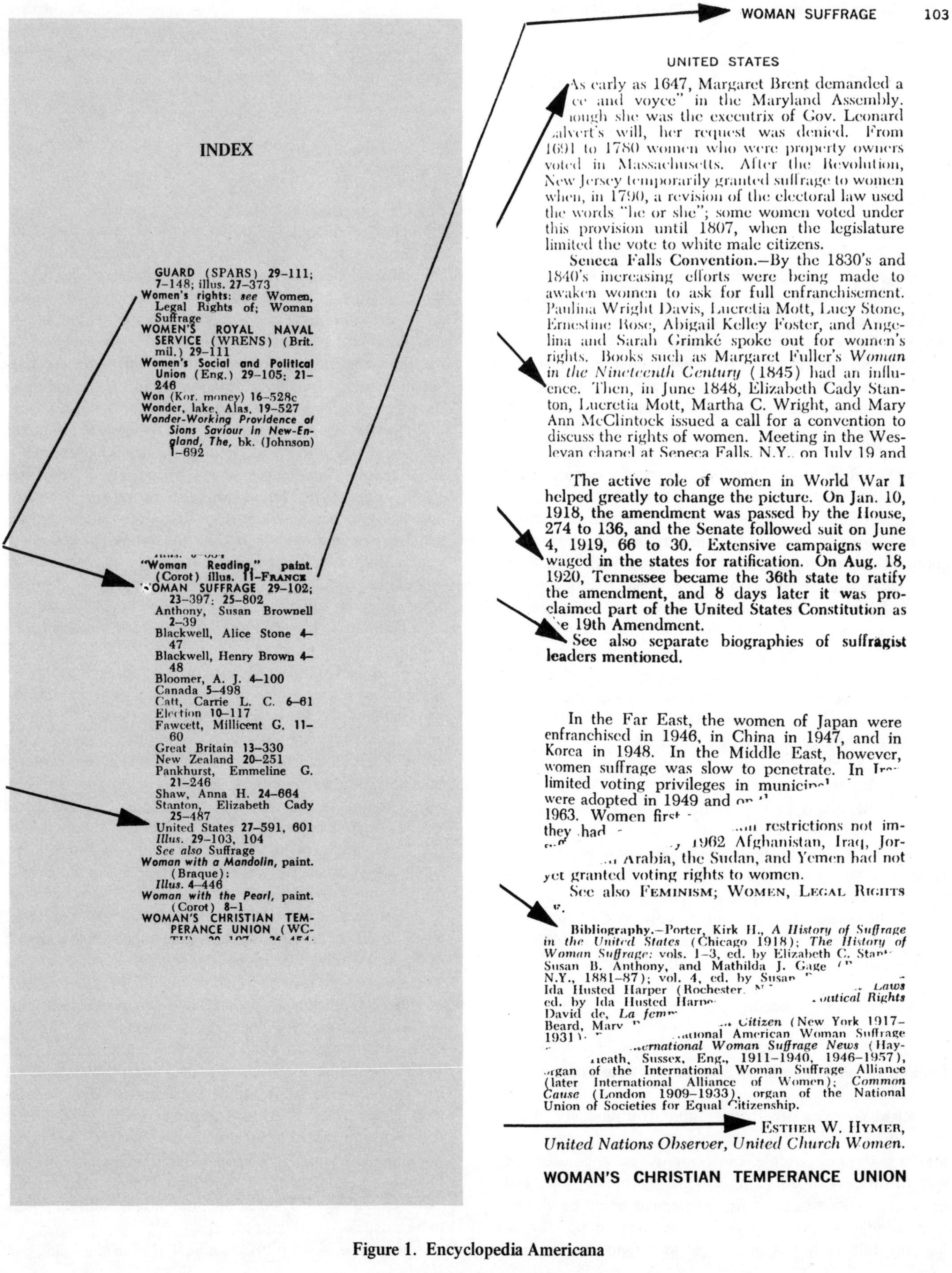
WOMAN SUFFRAGE 103

UNITED STATES

As early as 1647, Margaret Brent demanded a ce and voyce" in the Maryland Assembly. tough she was the executrix of Gov. Leonard alvert's will, her request was denied. From 1691 to 1780 women who were property owners voted in Massachusetts. After the Revolution, New Jersey temporarily granted suffrage to women when, in 1790, a revision of the electoral law used the words "he or she"; some women voted under this provision until 1807, when the legislature limited the vote to white male citizens.

Seneca Falls Convention.—By the 1830's and 1840's increasing efforts were being made to awaken women to ask for full enfranchisement. Paulina Wright Davis, Lucretia Mott, Lucy Stone, Ernestine Rose, Abigail Kelley Foster, and Angelina and Sarah Grimké spoke out for women's rights. Books such as Margaret Fuller's *Woman in the Nineteenth Century* (1845) had an influence. Then, in June 1848, Elizabeth Cady Stanton, Lucretia Mott, Martha C. Wright, and Mary Ann McClintock issued a call for a convention to discuss the rights of women. Meeting in the Wesleyan chapel at Seneca Falls, N.Y., on July 19 and

The active role of women in World War I helped greatly to change the picture. On Jan. 10, 1918, the amendment was passed by the House, 274 to 136, and the Senate followed suit on June 4, 1919, 66 to 30. Extensive campaigns were waged in the states for ratification. On Aug. 18, 1920, Tennessee became the 36th state to ratify the amendment, and 8 days later it was proclaimed part of the United States Constitution as e 19th Amendment.

See also separate biographies of suffragist leaders mentioned.

In the Far East, the women of Japan were enfranchised in 1946, in China in 1947, and in Korea in 1948. In the Middle East, however, women suffrage was slow to penetrate. In Ir... limited voting privileges in municip... were adopted in 1949 and ... 1963. Women first ... restrictions not imthey had ... 1962 Afghanistan, Iraq, Jor... Arabia, the Sudan, and Yemen had not yet granted voting rights to women.

See also FEMINISM; WOMEN, LEGAL RIGHTS ...

Bibliography.—Porter, Kirk H., *A History of Suffrage in the United States* (Chicago 1918); *The History of Woman Suffrage*: vols. 1–3, ed. by Elizabeth C. Stant... Susan B. Anthony, and Mathilda J. Gage (... N.Y., 1881–87); vol. 4, ed. by Susan ... Ida Husted Harper (Rochester, ... Laws ed. by Ida Husted Harpe... ...litical Rights David de, *La fem*... Beard, Mary ... *Citizen* (New York 1917–1931) ... ...ational American Woman Suffrage ... *...ernational Woman Suffrage News* (Hay...heath, Sussex, Eng., 1911–1940, 1946–1957), ...rgan of the International Woman Suffrage Alliance (later International Alliance of Women); *Common Cause* (London 1909–1933), organ of the National Union of Societies for Equal Citizenship.

ESTHER W. HYMER,
United Nations Observer, United Church Women.

WOMAN'S CHRISTIAN TEMPERANCE UNION

INDEX

GUARD (SPARS) 29–111; 7–148; illus. 27–373
Women's rights: *see* Women, Legal Rights of; Woman Suffrage
WOMEN'S ROYAL NAVAL SERVICE (WRENS) (Brit. mil.) 29–111
Women's Social and Political Union (Eng.) 29–105; 21–246
Won (Kor. money) 16–528c
Wonder, lake, Alas. 19–527
Wonder-Working Providence of Sions Saviour in New-England, The, bk. (Johnson) 1–692

"Woman Reading," paint. (Corot) illus. 11–FRANCE
WOMAN SUFFRAGE 29–102; 23–397; 25–802
Anthony, Susan Brownell 2–39
Blackwell, Alice Stone 4–47
Blackwell, Henry Brown 4–48
Bloomer, A. J. 4–100
Canada 5–498
Catt, Carrie L. C. 6–61
Election 10–117
Fawcett, Millicent G. 11–60
Great Britain 13–330
New Zealand 20–251
Pankhurst, Emmeline G. 21–246
Shaw, Anna H. 24–664
Stanton, Elizabeth Cady 25–487
United States 27–591, 601
Illus. 29–103, 104
See also Suffrage
Woman with a Mandolin, paint. (Braque): *Illus.* 4–446
Woman with the Pearl, paint. (Corot) 8–1
WOMAN'S CHRISTIAN TEMPERANCE UNION (WC-...

Figure 1. Encyclopedia Americana

find a number of references pointing at different aspects of the topic. The first volumes and pages listed (29--102; 23--397; 25--802) give the most general articles and they are listed in order of importance. In other words, in volume 29, page 102, you will find the main article on woman suffrage. While that is the article you will approach first, note the other general articles in volumes 23 and 25 and the article specifically on woman suffrage in the United States in volume 27. You will need to look at those too.

Volume 29, page 102, presents a signed article that describes the current state of suffrage in the world, the intellectual links with, and influences on, the women's suffrage movement, and finally, the historical record, arranged by country, giving some of the principal dates, legislation and people involved. You should note any of these that seem to you particularly pertinent: for instance, the earliest demand for women's suffrage in 1647, the date of the Seneca Falls Convention, and the date the final constitutional amendment passed, are all worth noting. Note also that on page 104 of the article shown in FIGURE 1, the writer carefully points you to the separate biographies of suffragist leaders the text has mentioned.

Note the bibliography, as shown in FIGURE 1, attached to the article: here is a beginning bibliography for you. Included here are many of the older contemporary accounts like Stanton, Anthony, Gage and Harper's six-volume *The*

History of Women Suffrage (New York: Fowler and Wells, 1881--1922), as well as some more recent works like Flexner's *Century of Struggle* (Cambridge, MA: Belknap Press, 1959).

Now is a good time to look at the other articles listed in the *Americana* index both under the general topic "Woman Suffrage" and under the more particular "Woman Suffrage -- United States." Scan each article for new information, new names, new dates, and perhaps most important, new bibliography.

You have looked at a general encyclopedia. Now look at what an encyclopedia that is more focused has to say. With the topic of the women's suffrage movement in the United States you can use an encyclopedia with a particularly historical approach (this is, after all, a history course you are writing for!), one such as the *Dictionary of American History*, 8 vols. (New York: Scribner's, 1976). Despite its being called a dictionary, this can really be used as an encyclopedia.

March right up to it and grab it by the index just as you did with the *Encyclopedia Americana*. But the wording is different in the *Dictionary* than in the *Americana*. As FIGURE 2 shows, again "Women's Suffrage" is not the topic, but this time "Women's Rights" lists no cross reference. But you are sophisticated enough by now to check also under "Woman's Suffrage" and your sophistication pays off in

WOMAN'S SUFFRAGE
   VII--314b; II--325b;
   III--91b--92a; VI--431a;
   VII--208b, 312a, 317a
Alaska I--77b
colonial settlements
   VI--434b
Equal Rights party
   II--457b, 457b
Greenback party   III--225a
League of Women Voters
   IV--126a
National Woman's Party
   VII--312b
Nineteenth Amendment
   I--95a, 297a, 297a;
   II--206a; V--97a
Progressive movement
   V--427a, 428a--b
Seneca Falls convention
   VI--262a
state government   VI--398b
voter turnout   V--108b
Washington State
   VII--248a
woman's rights movement
   VII--313b--14a
Wyoming   VII--346a
Woman's Temperance Crusade
   VII--312a
Woman Suffrage Association,
   National American
   III--91b, 92a
Woman with Dog (sculp.)
   VI--244a

WOMAN'S SUFFRAGE. Under English rule a few of the colonies, notably New York, permitted wo‑ of property to "vote their estates"; but ⸺.s, gave dence such suffrage as women ⸺ ᴠote; but, owing away, except in the ⸺ᴜons, in which blacks as its constituti‑ ⸺.ᴜ, suffrage was limited in 1807 to qu⸺ᴜ men.

Un the insistence of Elizabeth Cady Stanton woman suffrage was included in the program adopted at the Seneca Falls Convention in 1848. Efforts to secure the vote for women in connection ⸺.ᴜal enfranchisement of the Afro-Ameri‑ ⸺ᴜnt tactics. teenth and Fifteenth amen‑ ⸺ out for the amend‑ a split over poli‑ ⸺.ɢress the next year, and was Equal ᴘ‑ ⸺.ᴜr the national election of 1920 (*see* ⸺ᴜᴜn Amendment). Its most noticeable early ɪesults were laws in behalf of child welfare and of ᴍore rights for women.

[Carrie Chapman Catt and Nettie Rogers Shuler, *Woman Suffrage and Politics*; E. C. Stanton, S. B. Anthony, M. J. Gage, and I. H. Harper, *The History of Woman Suffrage*; Edward Raymond Turner, *Women's Suffrage in New Jersey*.]

MARY WILHELMINE WILLIAMS

FIGURE 2. Dictionary of American History

a listing of more than a dozen articles. The listings in the index under "Woman's Suffrage" direct attention to references on the topic made in articles on other subjects. The main article is in bold-face type. It will help to remember that indexes need to be watched, listened to, or understood, like all good tools.

In looking at the article on pages 314 and 315 (FIGURE 2) you will note that it is much briefer than that in the *Encyclopedia Americana* and more focused. The article mentions the connection between the movement for women's suffrage and that for "enfranchisement of the Negro," a connection that the first article in the *Americana* didn't make. But much of the other information you may already have picked up in the general encyclopedia.

Now look at the bibliography seen in FIGURE 2. It is very brief -- three items -- and gives no publication dates. But two items weren't in the *Americana* Bibliography, and you know from reading these summaries that most of the authors were contemporary witnesses. It is certainly worth noting.

With these encyclopedia articles you have begun to build your bibliography. Now is a good time to ask, how do you keep track of the items you are accumulating? To write them down on a sheet of paper has several disadvantages: the sheets tend to get lost among your course notes and, worse,

there is no way to keep them in order. If, for instance, you come across Flexner's *Century of Struggle* in another bibliography, you will need to read through all your sheets of paper to find whether you have already noted that book down.

The best way to keep bibliographic notes is on 3 x 5, or 5 x 8 cards. Cards can be kept banded together and they can be kept alphabetized for quick checks. They can be discarded and added to with ease. There are some students who keep their cards color-coded: pink for books, green for periodical articles, white for reference sources, etc. You can design your cards as you wish. One piece of advice: keep your method consistent so that you always know what you are looking at. FIGURE 3 shows a model card that notes all the bibliographic information (some of which was not in *Americana*, but was located in the card catalog and from the volumes themselves), the library's call number in the bottom left of the card and, very importantly, the source where you first found the book listed -- the *Americana*. This last will help you if you later want to verify your finding or get more information. You may also want to make notes later on this card about what the book covers, how useful you found it, even where reviews of the book are located.

When you find a bibliography on your topic or any new item for your list, whip out those cards!

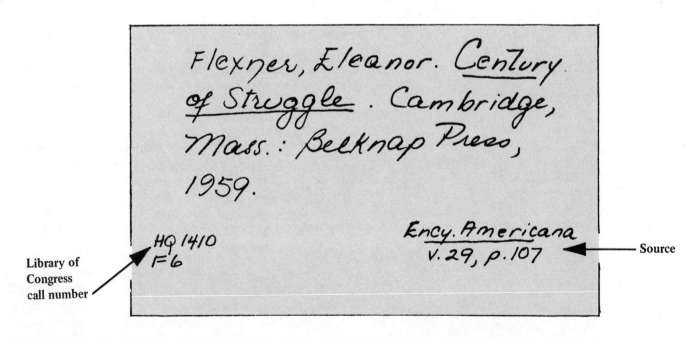

FIGURE 3. A card showing how to note an item of bibliography

Summary

1. Choose a topic that really appeals to you.
2. Begin your library search by reading summary discussions of your topic.
3. These summaries may be found in a variety of places: begin with an authoritative encyclopedia, exploring as you proceed the various subject headings used for your topic.
4. Whenever you have difficulty, ask for help. Your reference librarian is there primarily to help you.
5. Keep careful notes on file cards of each book, article and bibliography you locate. On these cards note the author, title, place, publisher, date and number of volumes of the work. Also note the library call number when you find it, and in what source you found this item listed so that you can find it again if necessary.

History, with all her volumes
vast, Hath but *one* page.
Byron, *Childe Harold*

Why Narrow Your Topic?

When beginning on a topic it is sometimes difficult to see the advantages of setting narrow limits. The more leeway you give yourself the more substantial your paper. Right? Wrong! Besides the limits the professor often sets to a paper's length, you are limited in the time you have to prepare it. Since it is not your dissertation you do not have several years to work on it. Even more important is the danger of superficial treatment of a topic. You are not writing that encyclopedia summary. You have been asked to research a problem.

In understanding the problem you must realize that there are many aspects of the history of women's suffrage that are of significant interest: For example, what are the events that led up to the final ratification in 1920? Who were the women, socially, politically, and personally, who emerged as leaders of the movement? What were the links between this movement and other reform movements of the day? What were the origins of the ideals behind women's suffrage? Who opposed voting rights for women and why? Only by giving a focus to your problem can you begin to understand the nature of the questions other authors are trying to answer in their writing. In other words focusing your ideas on the separate facets of the problem will help you to read intelligently and efficiently.

How to Narrow Your Topic

The summarizing articles in the encyclopedias and dictionaries, textbooks and reserve books you have used are a good place to begin the narrowing process. In looking, for instance, at the section of the main article on woman suffrage in the *Encyclopedia Americana* shown in FIGURE 4, you already found several leads offered to subjects that may merit closer scrutiny. One is the "doctrine of natural rights." What is it? and how does it relate to suffrage? A second is the mention of religious opposition to women's participation in politics. What religions objected and what were the arguments? A related topic is the economic interests that "wanted to keep women as a voiceless labor force." Who were these "interests" and what did they have to do with the labor force? And finally the paragraph mentions the "woman's vote as an ally of the temperance movement." How close was the alliance and what was the logical progression from temperance to suffrage?

Of all these statements perhaps the one that intrigues

you most is "Specific industries . . . feared the women's vote . . . . " You had heard before that the temperance movement was related to the suffrage movement, but how close

...men live;
...o eliminate other
...ically, suffrage came first,
...ad office next, and actual access to
...ffice still later.

The philosophy underlying the demand for woman suffrage was the doctrine of natural rights, and the woman suffrage movement was generally allied with other social reform movements, such as the abolition of slavery, temperance, and the extension of education. Although the movement was led primarily by women, it enlisted from the beginning the support of many men. Opposition took on different shapes in different countries. Political parties were uncertain of the effect of women's votes. There was religious opposition to their participation in anything that did not pertain directly to the home and the rearing of children. Economic interests wanted to keep women as a voiceless labor force. Specific industries, particularly the brewing and distilling industries, feared the woman's vote as an ally of the temperance movement. In general, established laws, customs, attitudes, and habits of thinking were slow to change, especially when they involved the acceptance of new ideas about women and their place in society.

UNITED STATES

As early as 1647, Margaret Brent demanded a "place and voyce" in the Maryland Assembly. Although she was the executrix of Gov. Leonard Calvert's will, her request was denied. F 1691 to 1780 women who were pr voted in Massachusetts. A New Jersey tempo when, in 17 A

FIGURE 4
Encyclopedia Americana

did the brewing industry come to fighting suffrage openly? What other industries fought it? Why? What documentation has been found for these statements? Your paper begins to have a focus.

Another source you can use to narrow your topic is bibliographies which frequently list books under topics, with topical subdivisions, helping you to focus on particular aspects. A good example of such a bibliography is Marie B. Rosenberg and Len V. Bergstrom's *Women and Society; A Critical Review of the Literature with a Selected Annotated Bibliography, 2 vols.* (Beverly Hills, CA: Sage, 1975--1978). The contents page, FIGURE 5, separates "Women as Voters" from "Feminism, Equal Rights," and further subdivides "Women as Voters." The authors go on to list another section, "Woman Suffrage," and subdivide that. Plenty of distinctions are made there, giving you many opportunities to narrow your topic. There are some fresh suggestions for new directions on your topic. For example, you might choose to look at the effects that the winning of the long battle had on voting patterns and on society. And you will note that the topic which had caught your attention earlier in the *Encyclopedia Americana*, namely the opponents to suffrage, is here given a separate subdivision listing 17 items (No. 1402 to No. 1418). Such a substantial listing can reassure you: "the opposition to suffrage" is a topic worth writing about. And looking at the list itself (FIGURE 5) underscores the fact that there is material on your topic – much of it contemporary with the events.

There are other bibliographies you can use, such as Albert Krichmar's *The Women's Rights Movement in the United States, 1848--1970* (Metuchen, NJ: Scarecrow Press, 1972), an excellent bibliography, but difficult to use for narrowing your topic, as everything is put together under one division, "Suffrage." Sue-Ellen Jacobs' *Women in Perspective; A Guide for Cross-Cultural Studies* (Urbana, IL: University of Illinois Press, 1974) is also good, but not helpful for

---

CONTENTS

Woman Suffrage: Opponents

Women in this country by their elevated social position, can exercise more influence upon public affairs than they could coerce by the use of the ballot . . . The woman who undertakes to put her sex in an adversary position to man, who undertakes by the use of some independent political power to contend and fight against man, displays a spirit which would, if able, convert all the now harmonious elements of society into a state of war, and make every home a hell on earth.
—Senator Williams (Oregon), 1866

1402. Anonymous. VOTES FOR MEN. New York: Duffield, 1913. 80 pp. Antisuffrage pamphlet which closes: "The yellow banner 'Votes for Women' is the last insult which the New Woman has offered to the intelligence of civilized man."

1403. Archer, Stevenson. WOMAN SUFFRAGE–NOT TO BE TOLERATED ALTHOUGH ADVOCATED BY THE REPUBLICAN CANDIDATE FOR THE VICE-PRESIDENCY. Speech of Hon. S. Archer of Maryland in the House of Representatives, May 30, 1872. Washington, D.C.: F. and J. Rives and Geo. A. Bailey, 1872. 20 pp.

1404. Beecher, Catherine Esther. WOMAN'S PROFESSION... EDUCATOR WITH VIEWS IN... Philad...

...ORE AND ...tton, 1925. 110 pp. Sees a decline in ... an eventual take-over of the world by women unless a new breed of men will reassert their old mastery.

1415. ———. WOMAN: A VINDICATION. New York: Knopf, 1923. 331 pp. Antifeminist account extolling women's negative qualities such as love of petty power, vanity, and sensuality.

1416. Smith, Munroe. THE CONSENT OF THE GOVERNED. New York: Academy of Political Science, 1914. Reprinted from Publications of the Academy of Political Science, vol. 5, no. 1. A rejection of woman suffrage on the grounds that the operation of government and acquiescence to majority voting decisions depends upon implicit threat of force. Since women are not fit to fight, they have no right to vote.

1417. Trevelyan, Janet Penrose. THE LIFE OF MRS. HUMPHREY WARD, BY HER DAUGHTER. New York: Dodd, Mead, 1923. 317 pp. Mrs. Ward, a novelist of note, was an ardent opponent of suffrage for women.

1418. Wright, Sir Almroth E. THE UNEXPURGATED CASE AGAINST WOMAN SUFFRAGE. New York: Paul B. Hoeber, 1913. 188 pp.

FIGURE 5. Women and Society; A Critical Review of the Literature with a Selected Annotated Bibliography

1771. _____. Woman suffrage and the Massachusetts referendum
of 1895. Historian, v. 30 (August 1968) ~~~ ~

1772. KENT, William. Concerning ~~~   ~~ (~~
viewp~~~~

~~~en 5. The ideas of the woman suffrage
movement, 1890-1920. New York, Columbia University Press, 1965. 313p.

1780. _____. Tactical problems of the woman suffrage movement in the South. Louisiana studies, v. 5, no. 4
(1966), 289-305.

1781. KRONE, Henrietta L. Dauntless women; the story of the
woman suffrage movement in Pennsylvania, 1910-1920.
PhD thesis, University of Pennsylvania, 1947.

1782. LABOR and woman suffrage. American federationist, v. 27
(October 1920), 937-9.

1783. LABOR'S position on woman suffrage. New republic, v. 6
(11 March 1916), 150-2.

1784. LA FOLLETTE, Fola. Will the women vote together? Independent, v. 86 (12 June 1916), 440-1

1785. LAIDLAW, Harriet Burton   ~~~
v. 56 ~~

17~~

FIGURE 6. The Women's Rights Movement in the United States, 1848--1970

Suffrage, Historical Feminism

Clark, David L. Brockden Brown and the Rights of Women.
~~ ~~ Pa.: Folcroft Press, 1912.
~~~~~ ~~~~ Akron, Ohio, 1851.
~~~~ ~~~~~~~ New
Fawcett, Millicen~ ~.
lished, 1912. Reprint, New ~~~~
Source Book Press, 1970.
Flexner, Eleanor. A Century of Struggle: The Woman's
Rights Movement in the U.S.A. New York: Atheneum,
1968.
Foster, G. Allen. Votes for Women. New York:
Criterion, 1966.
Fulford, Roger. Votes for Women: The Story of Struggle.
London: Faber & Faber, 1958.
Goodwin, Grace Duffield. Anti-Suffrage: Ten Good
Reasons. New York: Duffield, 1913.
Grimes, Alan. The Puritan Ethic and Women Suffrage.
New York: Oxford University Press, 1967.
Grimké, Sarah N. Letters on the Equality of the Sexes,
and the Condition of Woman. First published,1838.
Reprint, New York: Collectors Editions, Source Book
Press, 1970.
Hale, Beatrice Forbes-Robertson. What Women Want. New
York: Frederick A. Stokes, 1914.
Haskell, Oreola Williams. Banner Bearers. New York:
W. F. Humphrey, 1920.

205

FIGURE 7. Women in Perspective; A Guide for Cross-Cultural Studies

narrowing. In both you can, of course, find topics just by reading through the listed items (see FIGURES 6 and 7).

The card catalog also offers subjects and subdivisions. For instance "Women" in the card catalog may be subdivided into "Women -- Suffrage -- U.S." or, in some libraries, "Woman -- Suffrage," and leafing through those cards, like browsing through the titles in the bibliographies, may suggest to you new or more focused topics.

Another form of browsing for topics can be done right on the shelves. Once you notice a relevant book through your browsing in the catalog, locate it on the shelf. Then cast your eye around the area for other likely books. Use the indexes and contents pages of these to complete the process of honing your subject to a sharp point.

It would be time consuming to try to use all four of the suggestions above (summarizing articles, subject bibliographies, card catalog subdivisions and shelf browsing), for sharpening your topic. Use those that work for you, discard those that lead to dead ends, and commit yourself to a topic when you feel you have one that offers you enough important material without losing you in its vastness.

Summary

1. It is vital to avoid writing on a topic that is too broad, because a) you do not have time to write a book, b) you do not have time to do the extensive preparatory reading, and c) you do not want to be superficial in covering a topic.
2. Narrow your topic as originally conceived by using any of the following: encyclopedias, textbooks, and reserve books; bibliographies; subject subdivisions in the card catalog; and tables of contents and indexes of books.

Look for Bibliographies

If you are like many students, when you are asked where to look for books on any subject, you will answer, "In the card catalog." Did you know you are thereby tackling the most sophisticated tool in a library? As we will discuss in the next chapter, the card catalog requires some finesse on the part of the user. Is there an easier way to find a list of books on women's suffrage? Yes, there is, although in the end you'll probably finish in front of that card catalog anyway. But you will do well to begin by looking for some bibliographies on your particular subject. A good place to start looking for these is in two notable general guides to reference books. Your reference librarian can help you locate them. They are usually kept close to the reference desk for frequent consultation.

Use Guides to Reference Books

To begin with, you are clear that your subject is the opposition to women's suffrage. Going first to Eugene P. Sheehy's *Guide to Reference Books*, 9th ed., (Chicago: American Library Association, 1976) and checking the main volumes and the supplements, you will discover that for the subject "Women" and the subject "Suffrage" Sheehy is not very helpful. However if you use "History and Area Studies/ The Americas/United States" as a subject, you find at least two more general bibliographies which might prove helpful. Consult FIGURE 8. One item listed there is Henry Putney Beer's *Bibliographies in American History* (New York: Wilson, 1942), and the other is *A Guide to the Study of the United States of America* done by the Library of Congress (Washington, DC: Government Printing Office, 1960). Both are standards in their field. In checking these volumes on the reference shelves of the library you find that Beers, though old, gives you three or four bibliographies on women's suffrage. The latest of these is 1923, and you need to use the index to find them as there is no one section dealing with women's history. They may however prove very useful in tracking down contemporary material. The Library of Congress' *A Guide to the Study of the United States of America*, though newer, proves disappointing in its coverage of your area. In deciding it is not helpful, tuck the memory of it away nevertheless as a substantial, annotated, basic list for the study of U.S. history.

The second notable general guide which you can use as

UNITED STATES

Guides to research

Brooks, Phillip Coolidge. Research in archives; the use of unpublished primary sources. Chicago, Univ. of Chicago Pr., [1969]. 127p.   **DB9**

A manual for the beginning research ... archivist. Includes a ...
use." C...

→ Bibliography

quarterly with
... of authors and other main entries
...dex of personal names (including fictional names)
mentioned in the titles.   Z1361.C6A44

Beers, Henry Putney. Bibliographies in American history; guide to materials for research. N.Y., Wilson, 1942. 487p. (Repr.: Paterson, N.J. Pageant Books, 1959)   **DB13**

"Published January 1938. Revised edition March 1942."—*verso of title page.*

A classified list of more than 11,000 bibliographies including separate works, analytics, compilations in progress, and manuscript bibliographies, with author and subject index.

Covers many aspects of American history, including political, diplomatic, economic, military, religious, cultural, local, etc.
Z1236.A1B4

Bell, James Ford. Jesuit relations ... ...ed references. the library of Jame... ...., [1968]. 441p.   **DB27**

...two main sections: (1) a chronological survey, and (2) a country-by-country survey. Author index.   Z1609.R4T7

U.S. Library of Congress. General Reference and Bibliography Division. A guide to the study of the United States of America; representative books reflecting the development of American life and thought. Prep. under the direction of Roy P. Basler, by Donald H. Mugridge and Blanche P. McCrum. Wash., Govt. Prt. Off., 1960. 1193p.   **DB28**

Basically a compilation of works on various aspects of American civilization. The 32 chapters include such headings as: literature; geography; general, diplomatic, military, intellectual, and local history; science and technology; education; religion; economic life, etc. Nearly 6,500 numbered entries, most of them annotated, plus citations and evaluative notes for many related works not listed as numbered entries. Terminal date for some sections is 1955; others include publications through 1958.   Z1215.U53

FIGURE 8. Guide to Reference Books

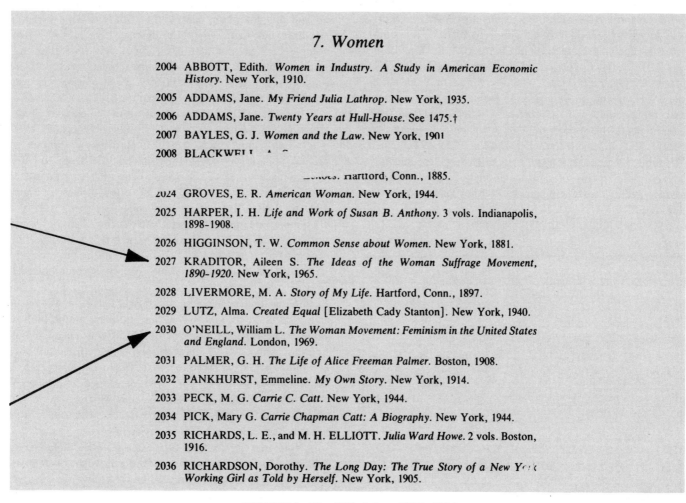

7. Women

2004 ABBOTT, Edith. *Women in Industry. A Study in American Economic History.* New York, 1910.

2005 ADDAMS, Jane. *My Friend Julia Lathrop.* New York, 1935.

2006 ADDAMS, Jane. *Twenty Years at Hull-House.* See 1475.†

2007 BAYLES, G. J. *Women and the Law.* New York, 1901

2008 BLACKWELL

‗‗‗‗. Hartford, Conn., 1885.

2024 GROVES, E. R. *American Woman.* New York, 1944.

2025 HARPER, I. H. *Life and Work of Susan B. Anthony.* 3 vols. Indianapolis, 1898–1908.

2026 HIGGINSON, T. W. *Common Sense about Women.* New York, 1881.

2027 KRADITOR, Aileen S. *The Ideas of the Woman Suffrage Movement, 1890–1920.* New York, 1965.

2028 LIVERMORE, M. A. *Story of My Life.* Hartford, Conn., 1897.

2029 LUTZ, Alma. *Created Equal* [Elizabeth Cady Stanton]. New York, 1940.

2030 O'NEILL, William L. *The Woman Movement: Feminism in the United States and England.* London, 1969.

2031 PALMER, G. H. *The Life of Alice Freeman Palmer.* Boston, 1908.

2032 PANKHURST, Emmeline. *My Own Story.* New York, 1914.

2033 PECK, M. G. *Carrie C. Catt.* New York, 1944.

2034 PICK, Mary G. *Carrie Chapman Catt: A Biography.* New York, 1944.

2035 RICHARDS, L. E., and M. H. ELLIOTT. *Julia Ward Howe.* 2 vols. Boston, 1916.

2036 RICHARDSON, Dorothy. *The Long Day: The True Story of a New York Working Girl as Told by Herself.* New York, 1905.

FIGURE 9. The Gilded Age, 1877--1896

a source of annotated information about bibliographies on your topic is *American Reference Books Annual, ARBA* (Littleton, CO: Libraries Unlimited, 1970--). This annual is a most useful way to find current reference sources. It can be used to keep Sheehy up-to-date. For example, volume 4, 1973, lists and describes the Krichmar bibliography, *The Women's Rights Movement in the United States, 1848--1970,* which you used in the last chapter. Krichmar's bibliography (see FIGURE 6) and other bibliographies like Sue-Ellen Jacobs' *Women in Perspective* mentioned in the last chapter (sample in FIGURE 7) are invaluable. Look particularly at items No. 1782 and 1783 in the Krichmar sample and at the Goodwin book in the Jacobs sample. There are many bibliographies listed under "Women's Studies" in the *American Reference Books Annual* and some more general , but useful, bibliographies under "History: United States." For instance, in this latter section the 1975 volume of *ARBA* lists De Santis' bibliography *The Gilded Age, 1877--1898* (Northbrook, IL: AHM, 1973) in the Goldentree Bibliographies in American History series. This is a series of bibliographies

specifically aimed at students like yourself. It is highly selective, carefully balanced among books, journal articles and dissertations, and arranged by topics in a helpful way. In FIGURE 9 from De Santis' book you will find a subsection "Women" listing many of the works we have already seen (e.g., Kraditor, O'Neill).

Use the *Bibliographic Index*

You should by now be beginning to develop a respectable list of books. There is one other list of bibliographies which you should become acquainted with before leaving these "bibliographies of bibliographies" (yes! that is what you have been looking at!). That is the *Bibliographic Index* (New York: H.W. Wilson, 1945--), a source both amazing in its scope and easy to use. Bibliographies are listed by their subject and they are listed whether they appear as separate books, as periodical articles, in pamphlets or at the end of a book. An incredible wealth of material is thus available.

Under "Woman Suffrage" in the 1972 volume, illustrated in FIGURE 10, is David Morgan's *Suffragists and Democrats* (East Lansing, MI: Michigan State University Press, 1972) which includes a 19-page bibliography. *Bibliographic Index* also notes that Sheila Tobias' "Study of Women," an annotated bibliography, appeared in *Choice* (vol. 8, Dec., 1971, pp. 1295--1304), a periodical devoted to selecting books for undergraduates. Under "Woman: Rights of Women" in the 1973 volume of *Bibliographic Index* appears the Krichmar bibliography you have already noted. And one year later it notes the section of *Women's Rights Almanac* (Bethesda, MD: Elizabeth Cady Stanton Pub. Co., 1974) called "Feminist Landmarks: An Overview of Historic Documents," a very useful listing of pertinent primary material. *Bibliographic Index* is a fruitful source of bibliographies on almost any topic.

FIGURE 10. Bibliographic Index

Consult the *Harvard Guide to American History*

Sheehy, *ARBA* (1975) and *Bibliographic Index* (1975) all will tell you about the *Harvard Guide to American History* (rev. ed., Cambridge, MA: Belknap Press, 1974), a two-volume bibliography that has earned, over its various editions, a reputation as one of the most scholarly and complete bibliographies in American history. Each edition has been edited by scholars of the highest calibre.

Look carefully at the arrangement of the *Harvard Guide*. One volume is arranged topically around subjects like "Westward Expansion" and "Intellectual History" while the second volume is arranged chronologically from the Pre-Columbian voyages to the 1960's. The table of contents of Volume I, as shown in FIGURE 11, offers at least two possible sections of interest to you: under "Politics" is listed a subsection entitled "Suffrage and Voting Behavior" and under "Demography and Social Structure" is a subsection entitled "Women." The first sounds promising but proves to have only material on general suffrage. The second, however, proves to be the mother lode. It can be found a little faster by looking under "Women and suffrage movement" in the index, also shown in FIGURE 11. Looking at the bibliography in FIGURE 11, you can see that after a general section comes a subheading "Feminism" and here are listed not only the books you have come to expect (Stanton, Flexner, etc.), but others you have not yet seen mentioned, like James J. Kenneally's "Catholicism and Woman Suffrage in Massachusetts," in the *Catholic Historical Review* which may throw some light on the anti-suffrage sentiment.

Note that the *Harvard Guide* is a selective bibliography with the authority of acknowledged scholarship behind it. In other words scholars have selected for you works they feel have the most to say on a wide spectrum of research in American history. Note also that it is admittedly thin on periodical articles and you will have to use other sources for those.

Note also that the *Harvard Guide* lacks a description of each item that would tell you whether, for example, Ira V. Brown's article includes any mention of the forces opposing the movement in Pennsylvania which would be of interest to you. Such a description would be an annotation, an abstract, or it might take the form of a bibliographic essay.

Annotated Bibliographies and Bibliographic Essays

An annotation is usually quite short and may be descriptive or critical. An abstract condenses the work itself into, maybe, one brief paragraph giving you the gist of the argument presented. A bibliographic essay is a lengthy discourse on the nature and use of a number of works on a topic. Eleanor Flexner gives you a bibliographic essay at the end of her *Century of Struggle* comparing, describing and weighing the books that are most useful to students of the subject. Tobias, in the bibliography you located through *Bibliographic Index*, illustrates both an annotated bibliog-

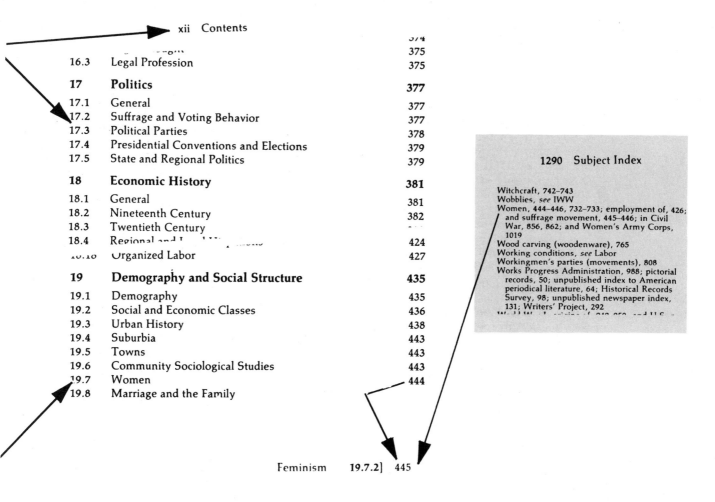

1290   Subject Index

Witchcraft, 742–743
Wobblies, *see* IWW
Women, 444–446, 732–733; employment of, 426; and suffrage movement, 445–446; in Civil War, 856, 862; and Women's Army Corps, 1019
Wood carving (woodenware), 765
Working conditions, *see* Labor
Workingmen's parties (movements), 808
Works Progress Administration, 988; pictorial records, 50; unpublished index to American periodical literature, 64; Historical Records Survey, 98; unpublished newspaper index, 131; Writers' Project, 292

Feminism   19.7.2]   445

19.7 WOMEN

19.7.1 General

Benson, Mary S., *Women in Eighteenth Century America* (1935).
Breckinridge, Sophonisba P., *Women in the Twentieth Century* (1933).
Cassara, Beverly B., ed., *American Women* (1962).
[...] *Modern Woman* (1952)

19.7.2 Feminism

Blumberg, Dorothy R., "Unpublished Letters, 1884–1894, of Florence Kelley to Friedrich Engels," *Labor Hist.*, 5 (1964), 103.
Board, John C., "Jeannette Rankin: Lady from Montana," *Mont. Mag. Hist.*, 17 (1967), 2.
Brown, Ira V., "Woman's Rights Movement in Pennsylvania, 1848–1873," *Penn. Hist.*, 32 (1965), 153.
Catt, Carrie C., and N. R. Shuler, *Woman Suffrage and Politics* (1923).
Degler, Carl N., "Charlotte Perkins Gilman on Feminism," *Am. Quar.*, 8 (1956), 21.
Flexner, Eleanor, *Century of Struggle: The Woman's Rights Movement in the United States* (1959).
Friedan, Betty, *Feminine Mystique* (1963).
Gattey, Charles N., *Bloomer Girls* (1968).
Grimes, Alan P., *Puritan Ethic and Woman Suffrage* (1967).
Irwin, Inez H., *Story of Woman's Party* (1921).
Jensen, Oliver, *Revolt of American Woman* (1952).
Kenneally, James J., "Catholicism and Woman Suffrage in Massachusetts," *Cath. Hist. Rev.*, 53 (1967), 43.
Kraditor, Aileen S., *Ideas of the Woman Suffrage Movement, 1890–1920* (1965).
[...] *Political Life Today* (1968).

FIGURE 11. Harvard Guide to American History

Of the "standard four," Flexner's *Century of struggle* is a comprehensive history based on the volumes of organizational material and the standard biographies of suffragist leaders. O'Neill's *Everyone was brave* is a provocative complement to Flexner arguing the thesis that American feminism failed insofar as it succeeded in becoming so broad-based and middle class that it alienated radicals of every stripe. Aileen Kraditor's *The ideas of the woman suffrage movement* (CHOICE, Dec. 1965) further illustrates the philosophical division between the "radicals" who argued from "justice" that women are equal to men, and those who argued from "expediency" that women are better and purer than men. Her companion volume of essays *Up from the pedestal* (CHOICE, Oct. 1969) is also important for any collection of suffrage material. Andrew Sinclair's *The emancipation of the American woman* (CHOICE, Feb. 1966), originally published with a title that would today seem very patronizing (*The better half*), is also comprehensive, critical, and good.

1. Example of a bibliographic essay

~ ~~ and the New York Times
~iv-volume *History*
~F Oct.

The Source Library of the Women's Movement series includes a number of volumes of out-of-print works relevant to the history of women. Among the most useful to an undergraduate library:

August Bebel's *Women under socialism* (1879) is mentioned elsewhere. Catherine E. Beecher's *Treatise on domestic economy* (1841) reveals 19th-century attitudes about woman's role as wife and mother.

2. Example of an annotated bibliography

Elizabeth Blackwell's *Pioneer work in opening the medical profession to women* (1895) is the autobiography of the first woman to receive a medical degree in the U.S.

Abigail Scott Duniway's *Path breaking* (1915) is discussed in the text.

Margaret Fuller's *Woman in the nineteenth century, and kindred papers relating to the sphere, condition and duties, of woman* (1855) incorporates many of the talks, articles, and letters by the noted American feminist.

~~rlotte Perkins Gilman's *The home:*
~ ~~~uence (1903) is a trea-
~ ~~~inist theore-

FIGURE 12. Choice

raphy and a bibliographic essay, as shown in FIGURE 12.

In assessing the works on the history of women Tobias uses an essay style. In describing the individual items in a reprint series she annotates each. Note how informative both methods are. The advantages are, again, authority, selectivity, up-to-dateness, and, in addition, detailed information. The essay tells you the place of the texts in the scholarship of the field. Note also some new books to add to your bibliography.

The most readily available bibliography, of course, is still the card catalog and we will investigate its use in the next chapter.

Another readily available, fruitful source of bibliographies is, of course, your friendly reference librarian. Don't neglect the obvious!

Summary

1. To find lists of books on your topic ask the reference librarian to point out to you the general guides and indexes to reference sources listed in this chapter, and the other useful bibliographies of bibliographies.
2. Cull these bibliographies for books that are particularly useful to you and note them on your 3 x 5 cards with a code telling you in which reference source you found them.
3. In this chapter you have learned to progress from bibliographies of bibliographies to the bibliographies themselves (e.g. De Santis' *The Gilded Age* or Krichmar's *The Women's Rights Movement in the United States, 1848–1970*), and from there to the books themselves (e.g. Morgan's *Suffragists and Democrats*).

I would I might be suffered to shewe my cardes.
Edward Campion, *Conferences Held in the Tower of London.*

Limitations and Difficulties of the Card Catalog

Because the card catalog seems like the best place to search, many students approach it before any other reference source in the library. Yet the catalog is fraught with tricks, turns, and difficulties.

The limitations and difficulties begin with the fact that each book is assigned, at most, a handful of subjects, maybe two or three. These subjects are often very broad, very general; e.g., this *Guide* you are reading might be searched under subjects for history, library, bibliography, research methods, student handbooks, etc. Which aspect do you use as a handle? And then the parts of books are not indexed, nor are the individual essays in an anthology listed. So that in a book on American history there may be an excellent section on suffrage, yet you will find the book listed in the card catalog only under the general subject of American history. Furthermore, there are obviously no periodical articles listed in the catalog. Yet periodicals are a vital, convenient source of research material. Finally, the card catalog gives little help in evaluating books -- though you will learn some tricks to reading between the card lines later in this chapter -- and many books in libraries are not "good" books boasting sound scholarship. They may be thin, questionable or even fraudulent.

A card catalog is usually simple to use if you need a particular book and know its author or title. You look it up in the author/title section of the catalog, copy its call number and fetch the book. The biggest difficulty comes when you try to find, through the card catalog, what books the library has on a particular subject. Then you must cope with the special language of subject headings, which is significantly different from spoken English.

The Language of Subject Headings

The language of subject headings is arbitrary. For instance, while "Sociology, Biblical" is a subject in the Library of Congress system, "Sociology, Historical" is not, but "Historical Sociology" is. While "Historical Sociology" is a subject, "Religious Sociology" is not; the subject is, instead, "Religion and Sociology." Similarly when we come to the topic of women, there is much arbitrariness, even inconsistency, built into the system.

You need to remember that all systems of subject headings (whether in card catalogs, periodical indexes or indexes to books) are arbitrary grids laid down over the mass of information, learning or scholarship. They are constructed in a way meant to help you get at the information you want and are more of less flexible depending on their construction. The Library of Congress subject headings comprise such a system.

In addition to the problem of arbitrariness of language, the card catalog has the problem of cross referencing. If the language is arbitrary or restricted the user will need a system of cues in order to locate the correct subject wording. If, for instance, you went looking for material on the fight for the women's vote in 19th century America, and if you chose to look under "Rights of women," it is important that you be directed to "Women -- Suffrage" if that is the authorized subject.

There are ways around these difficulties in any good subject system. The system we will discuss here is just one among several, but it is one used in most academic libraries in the United States. It is based on the *Library of Congress Subject Headings*, 2 vols., (Washington, DC: Library of Congress, 1975) and its supplements.

Standing in front of a card catalog, I often recall when I was little and my sisters wouldn't tell me a secret I wanted badly to know. Sometimes I wanted to know so badly, I would tickle them until they told the secret. The card catalog is like sisters: you have to tickle both to persuade them to abandon their high-handed reluctance.

Some libraries make life easier for you by listing cross references in the catalog itself. That is, when you look under the subject "Rights of women" you will find a card there that tells you to look also under "Women -- Suffrage."

Other libraries, to save costs, will not put such cards in the catalog, but will, instead, make the two large volumes of *Library of Congress Subject Headings* available for use at the catalog, together with their periodic supplements. Those supplements are important because the system is constantly changing, with new subjects being added and old ones altered, enlarged, or dropped.

Looking at a typical page in FIGURE 13, you can see the section which begins the detailing of subjects for books on women. Note 1 in the figure illustrates a "scope note," a brief explanation of what is -- and even what is not -- included in the subject. As note 2 indicates, beside the subject "Women -- History" is an LC classification number (HQ 1121--1172) telling you where the books that are primarily about the history of women, are shelved. Note 3 in FIGURE 13 shows that a subdivision of the subject "Women -- His-

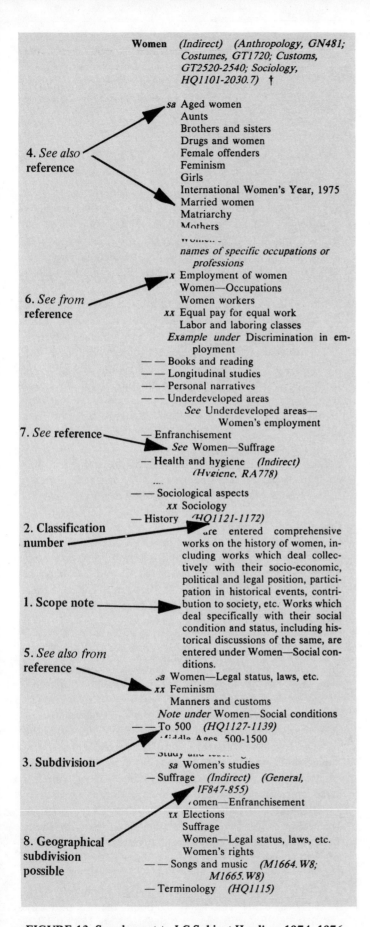

4. *See also* reference

6. *See from* reference

7. *See* reference

2. Classification number

1. Scope note

5. *See also from* reference

3. Subdivision

8. Geographical subdivision possible

Women (Indirect) (Anthropology, GN481; Costumes, GT1720; Customs, GT2520-2540; Sociology, HQ1101-2030.7) †

    sa Aged women
        Aunts
        Brothers and sisters
        Drugs and women
        Female offenders
        Feminism
        Girls
        International Women's Year, 1975
        Married women
        Matriarchy
        Mothers

        names of specific occupations or professions
    x Employment of women
        Women—Occupations
        Women workers
    xx Equal pay for equal work
        Labor and laboring classes
        Example under Discrimination in employment
    — — Books and reading
    — — Longitudinal studies
    — — Personal narratives
    — — Underdeveloped areas
            See Underdeveloped areas—
                Women's employment
    — Enfranchisement
            See Women—Suffrage
    — Health and hygiene (Indirect)
            (Hygiene, RA778)

    — — Sociological aspects
        xx Sociology
    — History (HQ1121-1172)
        ...are entered comprehensive works on the history of women, including works which deal collectively with their socio-economic, political and legal position, participation in historical events, contribution to society, etc. Works which deal specifically with their social condition and status, including historical discussions of the same, are entered under Women—Social conditions.
        sa Women—Legal status, laws, etc.
        xx Feminism
            Manners and customs
            Note under Women—Social conditions
    — — To 500 (HQ1127-1139)
    — — Middle Ages 500-1500
    — Study and teaching
        sa Women's studies
    — Suffrage (Indirect) (General, JF847-855)
            Women—Enfranchisement
        xx Elections
            Suffrage
            Women—Legal status, laws, etc.
            Women's rights
    — — Songs and music (M1664.W8; M1665.W8)
    — Terminology (HQ1115)

FIGURE 13. Supplement to LC Subject Headings 1974--1976

tory" is "Women -- History -- To 500." Note here that you are given further refinements of the classification number (narrowed to HQ 1127--1139). Note, too, that these subdivisions having to do with historical eras, are arranged chronologically ("To 500," "Middle Ages," "Renaissance" and "Modern period, 1600-- "). Notes 4, 5, and 6 are cross references. The "*sa*" note (fourth note) is a shorthand reference for "see also" and refers you to subjects that are related to, or are more particular aspects of, the same subject, as "Married women" is a more particular aspect of the broader subject "Women." You may wish to consult these related subjects to find books that are particularly on your topic. The "*xx*" (fifth note) refers you to other subjects of related or broader scope than the given subject. For instance, "Feminism" leads you to a subject of overlapping scope to "Women -- History." The "*x*" references (sixth note) you can ignore. They refer to subjects not used in the card catalog, but which users might mistakenly try to use. You need, then, to scan the "*sa*" and "*xx*" suggested subjects to note any that you may want to check in addition to the subject you have chosen, i.e., "Women -- History." The seventh note illustrates part of the answer to one of the problems we mentioned earlier: how do you know what subject to use for searching if the phrase you conceived is not used? If you searched under "Women -- Enfranchisement," the subject heading books here use a "*see*" reference to set you right: "Women -- Enfranchisement, *See* Women -- Suffrage." Further down you will, indeed, find "Women -- Suffrage" as a subject (note 8). The "Indirect" after this subject heading tells you that this subject may be further subdivided by geographical locality. The note "Direct" tells you the same thing. That is, you will be likely to find books in the card catalog under "Women -- Suffrage -- U.S." where your interest for this paper is primarily focused.

The Library of Congress, in response to criticism of the awkwardness and arbitrariness of its headings for women, has recently reconstructed that whole section of the subject heading book. In researching women's suffrage you may find that your library still uses the older heading "Woman -- Suffrage," you may find that it uses the newer heading "Women -- Suffrage," or you may find that it kept the old headings for older books and changed to newer for recent books -- in which case you would need to search both. Most likely the newer subjects are being used.

Judging Books by Their Catalog Cards

We have made the point previously that the card catalog helps little in evaluating books. Now let us revise that statement slightly. In going through the card catalog looking for books on your subject, you may have found one of the cards in FIGURE 14. If you know how to scan such a card quickly you can infer from it something about the author's authority, about the relevance of the book to your topic, the publisher's authority, the currency of the book, its scope and detail, and how useful it will be in leading you to other

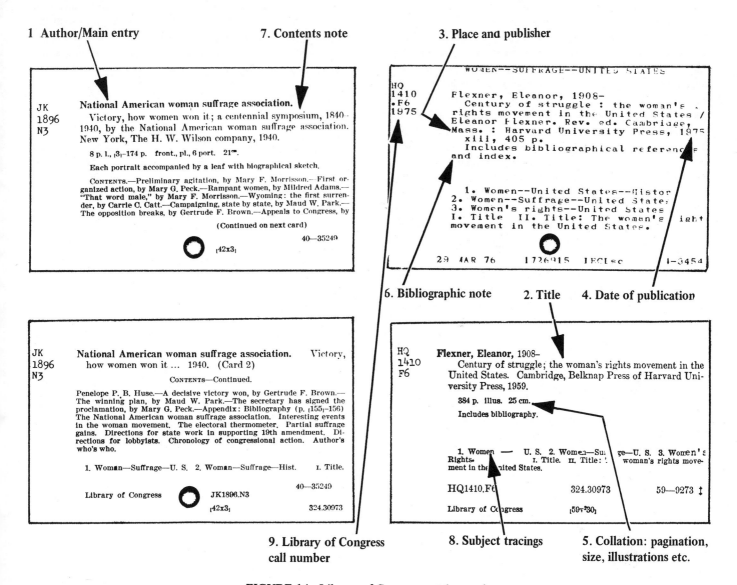

FIGURE 14. Library of Congress catalog cards

material.

FIGURE 14 shows four cards describing three books in the field of the women's suffrage movement. Note 1 indicates an author entry or main entry. You know from your reading of the encyclopedia article that the National American Woman Suffrage Association played a major part in the history of the suffrage movement as the two factions amalgamated. One aimed at a national constitutional amendment, the other at amendments of state constitutions. Sometimes your recognition of an author as a major scholar or authority in the field will aid you in selecting relevant works from the catalog. The title, too, can give you a fair clue as to the author's intentions. As note 2 shows, for instance, Flexner entitled her book *Century of Struggle,* then, in a helpful descriptive subtitle, added *The Women's Rights Movement in the United States.* Some publishers (like Harvard University Press in note 3) are known for scholarly publishing, others

for other qualities. The date of publication (note 4) will tell you much about the currency of the information contained in the book and about the historical milieu in which the author worked. For instance, a book on suffrage written in the 19th century will serve as a primary document, while one written in 1971 will serve more as a reflective secondary source. In addition, if you know that new documents shedding new light on your topic have been located since the publication of this book, you may want to get something fresher. On the contrary, if you know that in these years the really interesting work was being done in the area of your interest, this may be the book you want. While looking at dates you will notice that the Flexner cards in FIGURE 14 show different editions of the same book the first edition published in 1959 and the revised edition in 1975. A book which is published in more than one edition has probably proved its value, or at least its marketability. It is best to use the latest edition you can locate. Just below all this bibliographic information, is a line describing the physical aspects of a book: its pagination, illustrations and size (note 5). This line signals how substantial a book is, and whether or not it has illustrations or maps. You have already learned much from the card, but more is to come. The notes which are in the midsection of the card supply you with valuable insights into the book's usefulness to you. For instance, note 6 tells you that the author has listed her sources. These will often be the sources she has found most useful and thus provide you with invaluable aid in beginning your own bibliography. The card will frequently tell you how many pages of bibliography the author has included. On the other card, that for *Victory, How Women Won It*, the note is a contents note telling exactly what chapters are included in the book -- a real aid in deciding whether the book will be useful to you. This ends the first or descriptive part of the cataloging done on a book.

Now turn to the subject cataloging. At the bottom of the card, note 8 in our example, is a list of the subjects given to a book. These subjects not only give you some ideas for fresh subjects you can search in the card catalog, but also subjects you may have missed in the subject heading book. You may, for instance, have thought of searching "Women -- Suffrage -- U.S.," but may have missed "Women's rights" (the former subject was "Woman -- Rights of Women"). You have now decided you want the Flexner book, revised edition, you look in the upper left hand corner (note 9) for the call number, or shelf number, of the book and locate it in the library.

You have read an entire catalog card and already you have gleaned a fair amount of information about the book, simply by examining the author, title and publisher's statements, the edition and collation (physical description) statements, the notes and the subjects assigned.

Summary

1. The card catalog is limited because its language is arbitrary and fairly inflexible, it indexes the *general* subjects of books only, and it does not evaluate them. Use the catalog for what it does best -- locate books in the library -- and remember its limitations.
2. The language of subject headings can be complex. The major guide to the language of subject headings is *Library of Congress Subject Headings*. Use the headings marked "*see*," "*sa*," and "*xx*" to narrow your topic and to locate material on your topic. Do not use those marked "*x*."
3. Look first under the subject headings that most precisely describe your topic. Then use broader or related headings.
4. You can tentatively evaluate a book on the basis of its catalog card by noting the following: author, title, publisher, date of publication, edition, paging, descriptive notes, and subject headings. Read the entire card.

5. Finding the Best in Books

A few good books is better than a library.
William Ramsay, Gentleman's Companion

Finding the best in books, as in people, may require quite a bit of sifting. But when we speak of "the best" in books, unlike what we mean when we speak of "the best" in people, we generally mean the most relevant. For instance, in Morgan's book *Suffragists and Democrats*, which you found through *Bibliographic Index*, there are a number of chapters listed, but perhaps that which will most help you will be that chapter in Section III which is entitled "Liquor, Cotton, and Suffrage," where he claims that of the two campaigns linked to suffrage, the one aimed at temperance has received most discussion, while he argues that the campaign

for restricting child labor brought forth even more devastating economic hostility.

How do you locate those parts of books that are most helpful to your cause? How do you locate books that include such buried treasures? You could read entire books, but that is too time consuming. You might, then, skim books, but there are a great many of possible interest and even skimming everything is time consuming and unnecessary. As we suggested earlier, in Chapter 2, use the contents pages and the indexes of the books you browse. If these are well done they are of inestimable value.

You knew all this? Then *use* your knowledge to work systematically at developing your bibliography.

Using the *Essay and General Literature Index*

The *Essay and General Literature Index*, 1900 to date (New York: H.W. Wilson, 1934–) does what no other source does: it indexes collections of essays. Essays do not appear

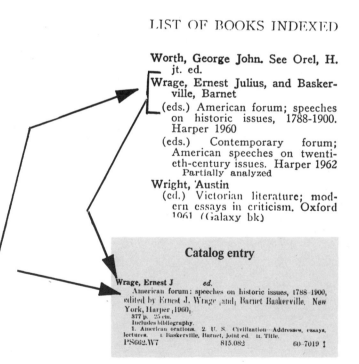

1. Essays by author

Beauvoir, Simone de
Stendhal or the romantic of reality; excerpt from "The second sex"
In Brombert, V. H. ed. Stendhal p147-56

About

2. Essays about an author

Cranston, M. W. Simone de Beauvoir
In Cruickshank, J. ed. The novelist as philosopher p166-82
McCarthy, M. T. Mlle Gulliver en Amérique
In McCarthy, M. T. On the contrary p24-31

About individual works
The second sex

3. Essays about individual works by an author

Mills, C. W. Women: the darling little slaves
In Mills, C. W. Power, politics and people p339-46

Woman—*Continued*
Ripley, S. W. D. Woman
In The Dial: a magazine for literature, philosophy, and religion v 1 p362-66
lic life

Suffrage

4. Essays on a subject

Anthony, S. B. For the woman suffrage amendment
In Wrage, E. J. and Baskerville, B. eds. American forum p318-32
Anthony, S. B. "The only question left to be settled now is: Are women persons"; excerpts from "Equal suffrage"
In Hurd, C. ed. A treasury of great American speeches p123-25
Brown, J. E. Against the woman suffrage amendment
In Wrage, E. J. and Baskerville, B. eds. American forum p333-42
Women as air pilots. See Women in aero-

LIST OF BOOKS INDEXED

Worth, George John. See Orel, H. jt. ed.
Wrage, Ernest Julius, and Baskerville, Barnet
(eds.) American forum; speeches on historic issues, 1788-1900. Harper 1960
(eds.) Contemporary forum; American speeches on twentieth-century issues. Harper 1962
Partially analyzed
Wright, Austin
(ed.) Victorian literature; modern essays in criticism. Oxford 1961 (Galaxy bk)

Catalog entry

Wrage, Ernest J   ed.
American forum; speeches on historic issues, 1788-1900, edited by Ernest J. Wrage and Barnet Baskerville. New York, Harper [1960]
377 p. 25 cm.
Includes bibliography.
1. American orations. 2. U. S. Civilization—Addresses, essays, lectures. i. Baskerville, Barnet, joint ed. ii. Title.
PS662.W7   815.082   60-7019 ‡

FIGURE 15. Essay and General Literature Index

in periodical indexes nor will you find separate essays from a collection listed in the card catalog. FIGURE 15 shows that you can locate material by an individual, about him/her, about his/her works, or about a subject, all by using the *EGLI*. In this case the subject of interest to you is "Woman – Suffrage." There are three items listed in the 1960–64 *EGLI* list: one, Brown's article, is of particular interest. The way to read this entry is thus: J.E. Brown has written an essay entitled "Against the Woman Suffrage Amendment" in a book entitled *American Forum* edited by E.J. Wrage and B. Baskerville. The essay runs from page 333 to 342. Obviously you want to locate the Wrage–Baskerville book. In the back of the *EGLI* is the "List of Books Indexed," as shown in FIGURE 15, where you can locate all the bibliographic information you will need. You can then check your library's card catalog to find whether it owns the book. In scanning the card you may notice (FIGURE 15) that indeed the subjects assigned to the book, "American orations" and "U.S. – Civilization – Addresses, essays, lectures," would not have helped you locate the Brown essay. The *EGLI* performs a unique function.

So there are three steps to use of the *EGLI*. First you locate your subject, second if you find books containing relevant material you check the full citation for those books in the "List of Books Indexed," and third you check your library to see whether it owns that book.

Locating the best parts of books then can be done through browsing in the contents and indexes of the books or through the *Essay and General Literature Index*.

Summary

1. A chapter or a few pages may be all you need from a book. Browsing will uncover useful pages that are inaccessible through the card catalog or through bibliographies. Browsing involves examining books which are shelved next to the promising books you found through the card catalog. Use their tables of contents and indexes.
2. The *Essay and General Literature Index* is used to locate essays and miscellaneous articles, most of which would otherwise have remained buried in the card catalog under broad subject headings.

A morsel of genuine history is a thing so rare as to be always valuable.

Thomas Jefferson, *Letter to John Adams.*

Scholars are fond of referring to "classics in the field" and "seminal works." There are also, certainly, bad books, misleading books and inadequate books. How can you, as a student with perhaps little experience in the field of history, know when a book is based on sound knowledge and when on shaky conjecture? Some of us have experienced the embarrassment of praising a study only to be told that its conclusions are derived from inaccurate premises. Because a book is in the library is no guarantee that it is good. Librarians are careful to build a collection that fairly presents all points of view. Furthermore a book may have been of high current interest when it was purchased only to be disproved or superseded later.

All this is to point out that you will want books of merit as well as pertinence to use for your paper and you will need more aid than that presented by the catalog card to recognize this. Judging the book by its appearance is not enough.

Judging a Book by the Company It Keeps: Bibliographies

A selective bibliography (as opposed to a comprehensive one), when well done, can provide you with a "best books" list of scholarly merit. *The Harvard Guide to American History*, which was described in Chapter 3, is an excellent example of this type of selective bibliography. It is useful, first, because it presents you with the most authoritative material as chosen by experts in the field, and, second, because it is selective, only listing the most significant and representative material on the subject. Neither of these advantages is to be found in a comprehensive bibliography listing all material written on a subject. Thirdly, it is useful because it is relatively up-to-date. These are the latest, as well as the best, books on the topic.

There are other bibliographies in which the items listed have been selected for scholarship and usefulness, bibliographies which are a help to you in selecting good books on your topic.

One way to discover whether a bibliography is comprehensive or selective is to glance at its introduction. This can also help you to assess the subject scope of the bibliography and what sorts of material were never intended to be included. For instance, dissertations are sometimes not included in a listing, or some authors may list just books, no journal articles. Another may include only those items published between certain dates.

Judging a Book by What Others Say About It: Reviews

You have used bibliographies to evaluate books; a second way to evaluate books is to look at how the scholarly world received them, i.e. through book reviews. The value to you of this sort of scrutinization is tremendous. The review is often written by an expert and may go into great detail over the pros and cons of a book and its place in the literature of the field. Reviewers often disagree on a book: their opposing views can present informative contrasts.

How do you find reviews of a book in which you are interested? There are several indexes to book reviews. Those you should know in American history are *Book Review Digest, Book Review Index, An Index to Book Reviews in the Humanities, Humanities Index,* and *Current Book Review Citations.* For critiques you have already learned to use the *Essay and General Literature Index.* In addition you should know about *Reviews in American History.*

Each is different. Let's look at each in turn. We'll look for reviews of Eleanor Flexner's *Century of Struggle* because it is the basis of your paper's approach.

Book Review Digest (New York: H.W. Wilson, 1905–) is more than an index; it also gives you very brief excerpts from the reviews it lists. FIGURE 16 illustrates the other information you can glean from an entry. Note that after the bibliographic information *BRD* often gives you a brief description of the book. Each digested review tells a little of what the reviewer said, names the reviewer where possible, indicates whether the review is overall positive (+) or negative (–) (though these indications cease after 1962), gives an exact citation where the review can be found and tells how long the review is (e.g., "500w" means 500 words). The illustration here lists some scholarly periodicals and this is actually the second listing of reviews for *Century of Struggle* that appeared in *BRD* (the first appeared in 1959). Since 1965, *BRD* will usually list a non-fiction book only if it receives two or more reviews in the eighty-three journals *BRD* covers, and those reviews have to appear within eighteen months following a book's publication. This often means that the scholarly reviews, which generally appear late, even as late as two or three years after publication, don't get listed. It is wise therefore to look at additional sources for scholarly reviews.

Book Review Index (Detroit: Gale Research, 1965–) currently indexes just under 300 periodicals and lists every review found in them. FIGURE 17 shows you a sample page. You will notice that there is no bibliographic information

FLEXNER, ELEANOR. Century of struggle;
the woman's rights movement in the United
States. (Belknap Press bk) 384p il $6 Harvard
univ. press
 324 Woman—Suffrage. Women in the U.S.
Woman—Rights of women 59-9273
For descriptive note see Annual for 1959.

 Reviewed by M. R. Dearing
 + Am Hist R 65:620 Ap '60 600w
"Miss Flexner's book . . . is a work of
meticulous historical scholarship. It is a serious
study, vibrant with human interest, of a significant social movement. It should interest
intelligent readers of either sex, as well as
sociologists who may find in it a useful adjunct
to the comparative study of social movements
of our times." E. K. Nottingham
 + Am Soc R 25:302 Ap '60 600w
"The outstanding qualities of the book are
the flexibility and elegance of the writing, the
variety and scope of the evidence, the vividness
of the detail, and the gathering force of the
drama which builds up firmly to its final climax
and unwinds briefly in the concluding chapter.
Men as well as women have much to gain from
the retelling of this revealing chapter of our
nation's history." K. H. Mueller
 + Ann Am Acad 328:178 Mr '60 500w
"The first balanced and scholarly account
of the woman's rights movement. . . The
seventy-year campaign for the suffrage is the
book's central theme, and Miss Flexner makes
a dramatic and absorbing story of it. . . She
can recognize an occasional flaw in the suffrage
heroines. At the same time, her gift of sym-
pathetic imagination brings the issues and
emotions of the past vividly to life. . . The
book has a few weaknesses. . . One might ask,
in view of the interesting account of Negro
women's problems and progress, why the immigrant woman does not receive comparable
attention. Miss Flexner's concern for the background of the events she relates is admirable,
but her treatment of historical forces tends to
be superficial. . . The author has used secondary works where she could, particularly
in the earlier sections. She has thoroughly
mastered this material and adapts it creatively,
though her treament becomes thin in areas
where basic research still needs to be done. . .
Her full account of the culminating decade of
the movement is solidly based on original
research." J. W. James
 + — New Eng Q 33:118 Mr '60 700w

FLEXNER, JAMES THOMAS. Mohawk baronet: Sir William Johnson of New York. 400p

FIGURE 16. Book Review Digest

Book Review Index

FLEW, Antony - An Introduction To Western Philosophy / Choice - v8
S '71 - p846
FLEW, Antony - An Introduction To Western Philosophy / Enc - v36
Ap '71 - p92
FLEW, Antony - An Introduction To Western Philosophy / Lis - v85
Mr 25 '71 - p384
FLEW, Antony - An Introduction To Western Philosophy / TLS - Je 4 '71 - p651
FLEXNER, Eleanor - Century Of Struggle / LJ - v96 - S 1 '71 - p2589
FLEXNER, Eleanor - Century Of Struggle / NYTBR, pt. 2 - F 21 '71 - p27
FLEXNER, James Thomas - George Washington. Vol. 3/ AHR - v76 - O '71 - p1220
FLEXNER, James Thomas - George Washington. Vol. 3/ Am - v124 - Ja 23 '71 - p74
FLEXNER, James Thomas - George Washington. Vol. 3/ BL - v67 - Ja 15 '71 - p398
FLEXNER, James Thomas - George Washington. Vol. 3/ Nat R - v23
Ap 6 '71 - p382
FLEXNER, James Thomas - George Washington. Vol. 3/ SS - v62 - N '71 - p278
FLEXNER, James Thomas - George Washington. Vol. 3/ VQR - v47 - Spring 71- p299
FLEXNER, James Thomas - George Washington. Vol. 3/ W&M Q, 3rd ser. - v28
O '71 - p667
FLEXNER, James Thomas - Nineteenth Century American Painting /
Choice - v7 - Ja '71 - p1500

FIGURE 17. Book Review Index

---

about the book, no indication of what the review says, and nothing to show who the reviewer is or how long the review may be. In fact the "*LJ*" shown is *Library Journal* and will be a very short review aimed at librarians selecting books, of little use to a scholarly paper. *BRI* does tell you where the review appears and on what page. The "*NYTBR*," for example, must be decoded using the "Publications Indexed" list at the front of the volume.

An Index to Book Reviews in the Humanities (Williamston, MI: Phillip Thomson, 1960–) is another index that now publishes virtually all reviews appearing in the close to 700 periodicals it covers. FIGURE 18 is a sample from the *Index*. The author's name and book title are identified. The asterisk indicates that the work was also listed in a previous volume of the *Index* and alerts you to search back. You should also check subsequent volumes of the *Index* because they continue to print reviews as they appear. The citation gives you the name of the reviewer, the periodical, the date, and the page where the review appears. Thus Carl N. Degler wrote the review that appeared in March on page 733. But in what periodical and what year? The "395" is a code for all this. In the front of the *Index* is a numbered list of the periodicals in which reviews appeared. FIGURE 18 shows the portion of this list explaining that the code "395" refers to volume 46, no. 4 of the *Mississippi Valley Historical Review*. You should be alerted to the fact that in 1970 the *Index* dropped virtually all historical journals and cannot be relied on for history after that date. Before then the *Index* is a very useful listing to use.

Humanities Index (New York: H.W. Wilson, 1975–) is the result of a 1974 split of the *Social Sciences & Humanities Index* (New York: H.W. Wilson, 1966–74), which has gone through a number of name changes since its beginning in 1916. Review articles appeared in the *Social Sciences & Humanities Index*, but were not always clearly labelled as such. With the split, book reviews have been gathered at the back in a section entitled "Book Reviews," an excellent source of reviews from a wide variety and number of scholarly journals. They are listed there only by author.

The citations as seen in FIGURE 19 are straightforward to read. In the example S.H. Strom wrote a review in the *Journal of American History*, vol. 61, Sept. 1974, pages 478 to 479, of Ross E. Paulson's book, *Women's Suffrage and Prohibition: A Comparative Study of Equality and Social Control*.

The other half of the split in the *Social Sciences & Humanities Index*, namely the *Social Sciences Index*, treats book reviews similarly. While you will find most of your material in *Humanities Index* where the major history journals are indexed, you will also find much material of interest to you as an historian in the *Social Sciences Index*.

Another recent list of reviews is *Current Book Review Citations* (New York: H.W. Wilson, 1976–). It is published in two parts, and gives an author (Part 1) and title (Part 2) approach to book reviews in over 1000 periodicals. The citations in Part 1 list the journal, volume, date and page where the review appears, and give the name of the reviewer

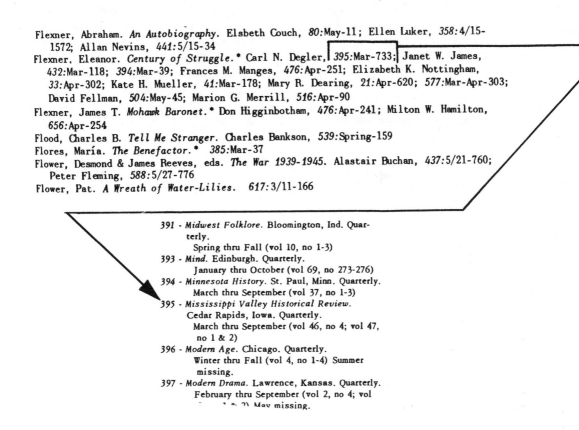

Flexner, Abraham. *An Autobiography*. Elsbeth Couch, *80:*May-11; Ellen Luker, *358:*4/15-1572; Allan Nevins, *441:*5/15-34

Flexner, Eleanor. *Century of Struggle.* * Carl N. Degler, 395:Mar-733; Janet W. James, *432:*Mar-118; *394:*Mar-39; Frances M. Manges, *476:*Apr-251; Elizabeth K. Nottingham, *33:*Apr-302; Kate H. Mueller, *41:*Mar-178; Mary R. Dearing, *21:*Apr-620; *577:*Mar-Apr-303; David Fellman, *504:*May-45; Marion G. Merrill, *516:*Apr-90

Flexner, James T. *Mohawk Baronet.* * Don Higginbotham, *476:*Apr-241; Milton W. Hamilton, *656:*Apr-254

Flood, Charles B. *Tell Me Stranger.* Charles Bankson, *539:*Spring-159

Flores, María. *The Benefactor.* * *385:*Mar-37

Flower, Desmond & James Reeves, eds. *The War 1939-1945.* Alastair Buchan, *437:*5/21-760; Peter Fleming, *588:*5/27-776

Flower, Pat. *A Wreath of Water-Lilies.* *617:*3/11-166

391 - *Midwest Folklore*. Bloomington, Ind. Quarterly.
 Spring thru Fall (vol 10, no 1-3)
393 - *Mind*. Edinburgh. Quarterly.
 January thru October (vol 69, no 273-276)
394 - *Minnesota History*. St. Paul, Minn. Quarterly.
 March thru September (vol 37, no 1-3)
395 - *Mississippi Valley Historical Review*.
 Cedar Rapids, Iowa. Quarterly.
 March thru September (vol 46, no 4; vol 47, no 1 & 2)
396 - *Modern Age*. Chicago. Quarterly.
 Winter thru Fall (vol 4, no 1-4) Summer missing.
397 - *Modern Drama*. Lawrence, Kansas. Quarterly.
 February thru September (vol 2, no 4; vol
 ` ? ?) May missing.

FIGURE 18. An Index to Book Reviews in the Humanities

when known. Part 2 (the title index) refers you to the citation in Part 1.

In the previous chapter you found that the *Essay and General Literature Index* included critiques of works. The example in FIGURE 15 showed that Simone de Beauvoir's *The Second Sex* was discussed by C.W. Mills in his own *Power, Politics and People* on pages 339 to 346.

In addition to these indexing sources there are two other, more immediate, sources you should not forget. The first is the annual indexes of the journals themselves which,

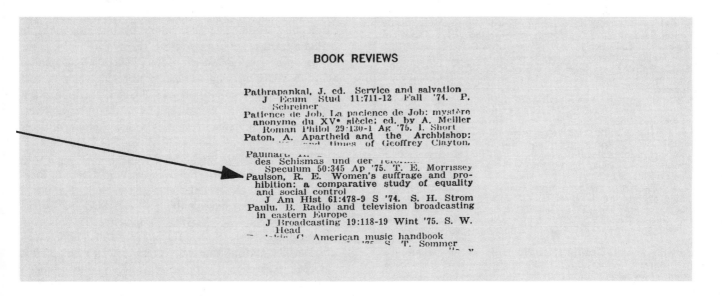

BOOK REVIEWS

Pathrapankal, J. ed. Service and salvation
 J Ecum Stud 11:711-12 Fall '74. P. Schreiner
Patience de Job. La pacience de Job: mystère anonyme du XV* siècle; ed. by A. Meiller
 Roman Philol 29:130-1 Ag '75. I. Short
Paton, A. Apartheid and the Archbishop: ... times of Geoffrey Clayton.
Paumai... ...
 des Schismas und der .... Speculum 50:345 Ap '75. T. E. Morrissey
Paulson, R. E. Women's suffrage and prohibition: a comparative study of equality and social control
 J Am Hist 61:478-9 S '74. S. H. Strom
Paulu, B. Radio and television broadcasting in eastern Europe
 J Broadcasting 19:118-19 Wint '75. S. W. Head
— ... C American music handbook
 '75 S T. Sommer "

FIGURE 19. Humanities Index

OF WINE AND WOMEN . . .

Anne Firor Scott

Ross Evans Paulson. *Women's Suffrage and Prohibition: A Comparative Study of Equality and Social Control.* Glenview, Ill.: Scott, Foresman and Co., 1973. viii + 212 pp. Illustration, tables, epilogue, and index. $1.95 (paper).

In this provocative little book Ross Evans Paulson argues that in the nineteenth and early twentieth centuries the "woman question" and the "temperance question" were aspects of an on-going debate in various countries on the meaning of equality and the nature of democracy (p. 7). He believes that these two social-political movements were "linked factors held together by the Victorian ethic" (p. 8), and he defines linked factors as "historical developments that are causally interrelated." He suggests that these movements can best be understood in a comparative framework, since both occurred in a number of different countries, and since equality meant different things in different cultures. Altogether he sets himself a formidable scholarly task.

The book opens with an examination of attitudes toward women's rights in the United States and in England between 1800 and 1840 ... author perceives differences which he ... value systems ...

... push for prohibition and for ... places.

Paulson concludes that "feminism, women's rights and women's suffrage and the correlated movements for temperance and total abstinence and prohibition [had] represented separate aspects of the search for equality and democratic social control in the accommodation of traditional social and political structures to the imperatives of industrialization, urbanization, and modernization" (p. 182).

As even this bare-bones outline suggests, Professor Paulson is not a man to fiddle around with small issues. His fertile mind throws off ideas like a Fourth of July sparkler. He is determined, as any first-rate historian must be, not to take the conventional wisdom for granted.

Yet there are serious structural problems running through ... First, he asserts that women's ... linked" by ...

... be carried through the

In collecting the data for this study Professor Paulson combed the secondary literature with admirable persistence, if not always with total understanding, and made occasional brilliant forays into primary sources. His lack of immersion in the primary materials sometimes leads him to misread his secondary sources—as he seems to do in defining what he calls "classic feminism," in his view of the differences in English and American responses to the women at the World Anti-Slavery Convention in 1840, in his perception of fundamental differences between Lucretia Mott and Elizabeth Cady Stanton, in his understanding of what he calls the restriction of economic opportunity for women in the 1830s, to cite a few examples.

Having said all this, I must nevertheless recommend the book. It is full of suggestive ideas. It is refreshing to find a historian who is willing to say straight out that the consumption of alcohol created real personal and social problems, and that we are not, therefore, required to find devious psychic causes when reformers made an effort to deal with those problems. It is helpful to be reminded that the United States was far from the first nation to enfranchise women, and that many societies besides our own experimented with prohibition. Margins of my copy are dotted with approving comments and notes of things to be examined further. Women's history has needed such a book: one that does not thresh old straw, does not rely on myth and wish, but broadens readers' perspectives and breaks new ground. Two cheers for Mr. Paulson, and let us hope that he and other scholars will proceed to test some of his provocative hypotheses.

Professor Scott, Department of History, Duke University, is preparing, with Andrew MacKay Scott, a study of the Nineteenth Amendment, scheduled for publication late this year.

FIGURE 20. Reviews in American History

as in the case of the *American Historical Review*, list the books and authors reviewed within each volume. The second source to be aware of is *Reviews in American History* (Pleasantville, NY: Redgrave Information Resources, 1973–), a periodical devoted solely to long scholarly review articles which often give additional information and opinions about the subject under discussion. You can see a sample from this scholarly review source in FIGURE 20, a sample reviewing the same Paulson book you found reviewed earlier through *Humanities Index*.

Judging a Book by Its Pedigree: Biography

Another clue to the possible merit, or lack of it, of a book is the scholarship, authority and reputation of its author. One way to find this sort of informations is by looking for biographical material. Biographical material is tricky to find and the clearest way to locate it is by asking yourself a set of questions: is he/she American, British, French, etc? Is he/she alive or dead? To each of these questions there are only three possible answers: yes, no or don't know. The questioning process is so precise, it can be drawn as a flowchart that will lead you inexorably to a particular set of reference sources.

There are some sources that are so standard, you should learn them by heart. Some of these standards are *Who's Who, Who's Who in America, Who Was Who, Who Was Who in America, Directory of American Scholars, Current Biography, Contemporary Authors, New York Times Index, National Cyclopaedia of American Biography, Notable American Women*, and last, and most important, the *Dictionary of American Biography*.

Before launching into discussions of these, there is one overall source comparable to *Bibliographic Index* which we talked about in Chapter 3. *Biography Index* (New York: H.W. Wilson, 1949–) is a bibliography of biography, a list of biographies, as they appear in books, in collective works, in periodical articles etc. As you can see in FIGURE 21, the format is straightforward and points you to a biography of Judge Ward Hunt, who summarily directed a jury to find Susan B. Anthony guilty in her 1873 trial for registering and voting in Rochester. This biography might otherwise have remained hidden, gathered as it is with a number of other biographies.

Returning to our list of basic sources, let's begin with the final item in the list, the *Dictionary of American Biography*, 20 vols. and supplements (New York: Scribner's, 1928–1936, with supplements 1944–). Modeled on the British *Dictionary of National Biography*, 21 vols. and supplements (New York: Macmillan, 1908–1909, with supplements, Oxford University Press, 1927–), the *DAB* is scholarly, presents a wealth of information, and includes a bibliography of sources by and about the subject. Note that, like the *DNB*, the subject must be dead to appear in the *DAB*. Without doubt this is one of the best sources of biographical material about prominent American figures, no

memoirs.
bibliog por autog...

HUNT, Robert Walter, 1904-19..
Obituary
Am Med Assn J 146:664 Je 16 '51
N Y Times p25 Ap 2 '51

HUNT, Roy Arthur, 1878- insurance executive
Col. Roy Arthur Hunt retires after fifty remarkable years in publishing. por W Underw 163:1140-1+ N 18 '50

HUNT, Ward, 1810-1886, Supreme Court justice
Campbell, Tom Walter. Four score forgotten men. Pioneer pub. co. '50 p244-6 por

HUNT, Westley Marshall, 1888-1950, surgeon
Obituary
Am Med Assn J 143:1356 Ag 12 '50
N Y Times por p29 Je 29 '50

HUNT, William, 1842-1931, English historian
Biography. DNB 1931-1940:455-6 '49

– William Morris, 1824-1879, painter
William Morris Hunt and his
Mag Art 43:144-50 Ap '50

...ord. E. L.

FIGURE 21. Biography Index

longer living, in all fields.

Notable American Women, 1607--1950, 3 vols. (Cambridge, MA: Belknap, 1971) is modeled on both the *DNB* and the *DAB*, yet grew out of a recognition of those sources' limitations: they do not adequately cover many of the figures who contributed a great deal to history. *Notable American Women* is just as scholarly as its models and provides a new depth of biographical material about women. The third volume includes a list of biographies classified by occupation or field. The introduction in volume 1 is an excellent historical survey of women in American history written by Janet Wilson James.

The *National Cyclopaedia of American Biography* (Clifton, NJ: James T. White, 1893-- with current volumes A-- , 1930–) is more comprehensive than any of the above, but the biographies are less scholarly, are considerably shorter, do not provide bibliographies, and are arranged a little differently. (You need to use the index to find your subject).

The New York Times Index, 1851 to date (New York: New York Times Co., 1913–) goes back as far as the mid-19th century and lists not only biographical articles (some action-oriented news stories, some called profiles), but also obituaries, sometimes of considerable length, that recount and weigh the subject's actions and attainments. FIGURE 22 shows you how to read a *NYTI* citation, in this case an obituary notice for Elizabeth Cady Stanton. Note particularly that the year is not mentioned (you get that from the spine of the volume you are using), and that both page and column number are given to aid you in locating the story. Though the typeface has changed, the current volumes of the *NYTI* give you similar information: the gist of the article, its date, page, and column.

Contemporary Authors: A Bio--Bibliographical Guide to Current Authors and Their Works (Detroit: Gale, 1962–) is a series that, as the subtitle indicates, presents the usual biographical along with incidental material, (e.g., hobbies), and a list of the author's best-known works. You can use the cumulated indexes in alternate volumes to locate an author.

Current Biography (New York: H.W. Wilson, 1940–) has one problem: earlier volumes become out of date and are difficult to keep truly "current" or "contemporary." *Current Biography* seldom attempts to up-date its sketches, which makes some sense as their subjects are included for their newsworthiness and prominence at the time of writing. Obituaries of former subjects, including those in the *New York Times* and elsewhere, are noted. The biographies are fairly long, include a picture, and finish with a brief list of other sources of information on the biographies. Indexes cumulate for ten years, making searches a little easier to conduct.

The *Directory of American Scholars*, 7th ed., 4 vols. (New York: Bowker, 1978) is a source for short *Who's Who*-type biographical information on some 38000 scholars around the country covering the fields of History, English, Speech, Drama, Foreign Languages, Linguistics, Philology, Philosophy, Religion, and Law. It is divided into four volumes, the most useful to you being volume 1, History. Volume 4 has an index.

Who's Who in America (Chicago: Marquis Who's Who, 1899–) and its companion *Who Was Who in America* (Chicago: Marquis Who's Who, 1942–), *Who's Who* (New York: St. Martin's Press, 1906–) and its sister *Who Was Who* (London: Adam and Chas. Black, 1920--) give the briefest, but detailed, biographical sketches of a wide number of subjects, covering their birth, education, affiliations, interests, current location, etc. *Who's Who in America* and *Who Was Who in America* obviously cover American notables, while *Who's Who* and *Who Was Who* cover prominent figures worldwide but with special emphasis on Britain. Since the historical volumes go back a fair way (in the case of *Who Was Who in America*, to 1607, or *Who Was Who*, to 1897), there is quite a bit of ground that can be covered using these four titles.

–Canad...
Sport, Texas..........
–Hector Ames letter..........
Squires, E. L.; abductor caught.Oct. 6–...
Staehle, D. H.; sketch; Kriegsspiel..
Aug. 26–2-5
Stamps; Vienna conf..........Sept. 28–5-2
–Cape of Good Hope £350.......Nov. 2–4-4
Stanley, Gen D. B.; heirs sue Mut.
Res. Fund....................Sept. 11–8-6
Stanton, Eliz. Cady; dies.......Oct. 27–1-3
–Funeral.....................Oct. 30–9-4
–N. Y. memorial meeting......Nov. 20–9-5
Stanton, Walter; fails.........Sept. 30-12-2
Staples, C. E.; sued by Mrs. Singer..
Oct. 24–7-5
Staten Is. elec. cos. sold........Aug. 7–2-4
–Ferry fight; B. & O. vs. Standard
Oil.......................July 2, 3-16-1
–Rogers's 13 minute boat......July 8–1-2
–Trolley problems.............Aug. 3-26-2
–Rogers syndicate plans....Nov. 12-16-3
–High school cornerstone......Dec. 21-26-6
...ckler, Judge Alfred; portrait given
..................Oct. 4–6-3
......Oct. 7–3-3
... 21–6-3

1. Date (Oct. 27)
2. Page (1)
3. Column (3)

FIGURE 22. New York Times Index

Keep in mind that you can also use the dust jacket of a book to obtain more information about who the author is. Similarly, there are often squibs about an author attached to a scholarly article – often only institutional affiliation, but sometimes going further to include previous work and biographical information.

Putting together two or more of these sources, you can locate some, albeit frequently scanty, information as to the scholarship, authority and reputation of an author.

Judging a Book by What It Is: Using Judgment

In all this we have judged the book mainly by external means. Do not let this lead you into the sin of "judging a book by its cover." Judge rather the book within, and only you can do that completely to your own satisfaction. While reviews and reputation have to play a part in your final analysis, your own appreciation and knowledge of the subject, and of your needs, must play a part too.

Judgment, in all these matters of quality, is important if difficult. Ambrose Bierce's *Devil's Dictionary* defines history as "An account mostly false, of events unimportant, which are brought about by rulers mostly knaves, and soldiers mostly fools."

Summary

1. The construction of a sound, selective bibliography for your paper requires some evaluation of the books that go into it.
2. The use of bibliographies, particularly selective and annotated ones, can help you to choose those most valuable to your task.
3. Book reviews offer information about how a work was received by the scholarly world. Each book review index offers special advantages and disadvantages in locating helpful reviews.
4. To find out who an author is you will want to find biographical information. You can try the standard biographical sources, then move to *Biography Index* to locate biographies hidden in books and periodicals.
5. Finally, you will want to assess the work yourself through careful reading and weighing.

Histories are a kind of dis-
tilled newspapers.
Carlyle, *On Heroes and Hero-
Worship.*

In the literature of a field, oldest is not always best, although history is one of the few fields where old comes very
close to being better. There are times, however, when you
will want recent material, notably in order to interpret or
update older material, to compare a more recent happening
to an older one, or to research topics of current interest.
For instance, women's suffrage has recently been the subject
of fresh research, reflecting the growth in women's studies,
and you might want to look at some of these newer views.
Or you may want to include in your paper a brief comparison of the interest behind the anti-Equal Rights Amendment
movement and that behind anti-suffrage sentiment at the
turn of the century.

Current research in history appears in periodicals and
the road into periodical literature is by periodical indexes
and abstracts. Those most useful to history can be divided
into four categories: general indexes, history indexes, abstracts, and newspaper indexes.

General Indexes

The first of our categories of indexes and abstracts
are the general indexes. Of these perhaps four are especially
worthy of note. They are *Readers' Guide to Periodical
Literature, Humanities Index, Bulletin of the Public Affairs
Information Service*, and *Social Sciences Citation Index*.

The *Readers' Guide to Periodical Literature* (New York:
H.W. Wilson, 1905–) may have become familiar to you in
high school. While it covers primarily popular periodicals, it

is useful to the historian particularly because it supplies a
contemporary viewpoint on events as they occurred and because it indexes a few of the major history periodicals, like
American Historical Review. Along with its predecessors,
Poole's Index to Periodical Literature, 6 vols. (v. 1, Boston:
Osgood, 1882; vols. 2–6, Boston: Houghton, 1888–1908)
which covers the years 1802 to 1906, and *Nineteenth Century Readers' Guide to Periodical Literature*, 2 vols. (New
York: H.W. Wilson, 1944) which covers 1890 to 1922, *R.G.*
gives you excellent coverage of the contemporary viewpoint
on events of the last two centuries.

For the scholarly viewpoint on events, you will find
more material in *Humanities Index*, which was formerly
Social Sciences & Humanities Index, International Index,
and *Readers' Guide to Periodical Literature Supplement*,
whose acquaintance you made in Chapter 6 in the search for
book reviews. Its primary function is to index articles in
periodicals and it is well worth using because it covers the
most important scholarly history periodicals, those most
likely to be in an undergraduate library. FIGURE 23 shows
a typical entry under the subject "Woman – Suffrage –
United States" and an article apparently describing the inter-
action of three aspects of 19th century reform within a narrow space of time. The illustration explains how to read the
citation. You should note that these indexes often abbreviate
the title of the periodical. Always check the title in the list of
periodicals at the beginning of the volume, before you search
the card catalog for the periodical. Many a title owned by a
library has been overlooked by not paying attention to
"the," "for" or "of" in the name of the periodical, e.g.,

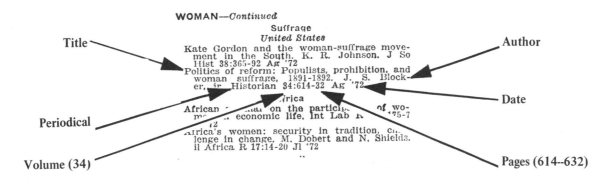

FIGURE 23. Social Sciences & Humanities Index

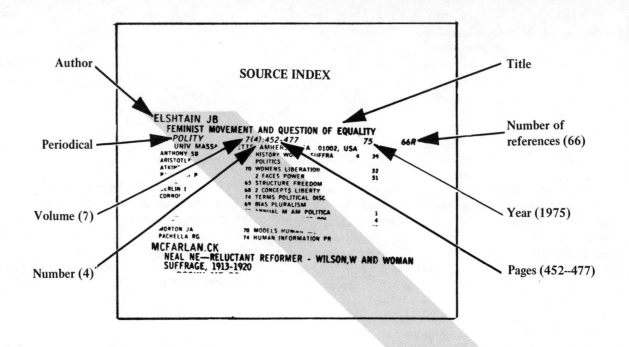

FIGURE 24. Social Sciences Citation Index

don't overlook "the" in *Journal of the History of Ideas*.

The *Bulletin of the Public Affairs Information Service* (New York: Public Affairs Information Service, 1920–), better know as *PAIS*, scans a great deal more material and types of material than other indexing services: it selectively indexes not only periodical titles, but also books, pamphlets, reports and even major government documents, often alerting you to important hearings in Congress.

The most unusual index you will have to use is the *Social Sciences Citation Index, 1972--* (Philadelphia: Institute for Scientific Information, 1974–). Looking at FIGURE 24, you can see that it begins in a fairly regular way with a list of current journal articles alphabetically arranged by author. This is the Source Index and on closer inspection it reveals some unusual features. First, it is clearly computerized. Second, it tells you how many footnotes the author has used. Third, the institutional affiliation of the author is given, which tells you something perhaps about the nature of the article. Fourth, it lists all the articles upon which this research is based; that is, it lists the author's footnotes in alphabetical order.

There is a subject index to this recent material; a sample is shown in FIGURE 24. This is what *SSCI* calls its Permuterm Subject Index and again, a close look shows its unusual features. First, this is a computerized index. It is made up by permuting, or combining, every two significant terms in the title of an article. So if titles are at all descriptive, you should be able to find articles, particularly if you are a little creative about looking under a variety of words that might appear in any article of interest to you. In FIGURE 24 the word "suffrage" is a main search term and combined with the word "woman" it points to an article by C.K. McFarland and N.E. Neal, "The Reluctant Reformer: Woodrow Wilson and Woman Suffrage, 1913–1920," in the *Rocky Mountain Social Science Journal*, vol. 11, April 1974, pp. 33–43. This you find cited in the Source Index volume, which is the author listing of current articles. Now comes the third and most remarkable section of *SSCI*. The Citation Index is a listing of every book, article, etc., no matter how old, that has been cited in the current literature. FIGURE 24 illustrates this section and shows its arrangement to be alphabetical by author. It is also computerized. Look at the section under Kraditor. Note that there are three Kraditors listed as authors and note also that the three are in fact one; the Aileen S. Kraditor whose work, *Ideas of the Woman Suffrage Movement, 1890--1920*, you found listed in the Krichmar bibliography, (FIGURE 6), in DeSantis' bibliography, (FIGURE 9) and in the *Harvard Guide*, (FIGURE 11). Why is Kraditor shown in three different ways in the sample of *SSCI* in FIGURE 24? This is a function of the computerized index. The computer makes no connection between a Kraditor that one author cites as "Kraditor," another as "Aileen Kraditor" and another as "Aileen S. Kraditor." It's an illustration of the care that has to be taken in using a computerized index. This same book may have several different editions and you should therefore also be careful when using the index to check the various editions, each of which is listed separately by date of publication. Note, for instance, the three separate citings in the same sample of Jonathan Kozol's book, *Death at an Early Age*.

How best to use the Citation Index? It is an exciting way for you to get into the bibliography on a topic *when you have already found a book or article that is directly on your topic*. Taking Kraditor's book as an example: if *Ideas of the Woman Suffrage Movement, 1890--1920*, with its major section on antisuffragism, is precisely the book you want, you can use her footnotes, as well as her excellent bibliography, to get yourself into the prior research in the field and into the primary documents. You can use the Citation Index of the *SSCI* to get yourself into the work that has been done since her book, the work that has based its research on her findings, the work that has cited her. J.B. Elshtain, the author highlighted in FIGURE 24, is one such and is worth looking up. Lawyers and scientists have been using the citation method of tracing literature for some time. With the advent of *SSCI* the social scientists (which occasionally includes historians!) have a similar opportunity. Using the footnote and citation method of searching for material introduces you to a new search strategy about which you can read more in Appendix I.

SSCI is an expensive reference source which is not owned by most college libraries. Even so, it is worth knowing about because you may visit a university which has it, or you may go to an advanced degree in history, at which point it will prove invaluable.

History Indexes

C.R.I.S.; The Combined Retrospective Index Set to Journals in History, 1838--1974, 11 vols. (Washington, DC: Carrollton, 1977) is a monumental work that indexes 243 English language history periodicals. Volumes 1 to 4 cover world history and 5 to 9 cover United States history, with 10 and 11 indexing authors. Some 150,000 articles are arranged in the nine subject volumes under 342 broad categories, which are further subdivided by key words taken from the titles of articles.

When you look in the section headed "United States Politics and Political Philosophy," as shown in FIGURE 25, you find several articles on woman's suffrage cited under "woman" and "suffrage," as key words. One of the "reference titles" (not necessarily the title of the article) is "Woman Suffrage," which is by E.A. Taylor, published in 1959, in volume 15, starting on page 17 of journal number 20. To find out the title of journal number 20, look inside the front cover. As shown, number 20 is *Arkansas Historical Quarterly*.

Because *C.R.I.S.; The Combined Retrospective Index Set to Journals in History* gives such quick access to so many journals, it is a great time-saver. The unpleasant alternative is to dig through many volumes of several periodical indexes, such as the *International Index*, and even then you will not cover as many titles as are in *C.R.I.S.* However, *C.R.I.S.* has

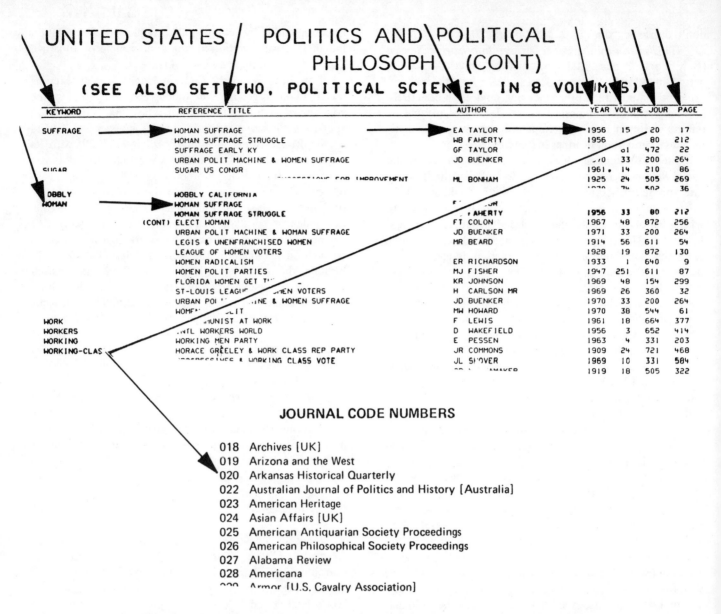

FIGURE 25. C.R.I.S.; The Combined Retrospective Index Set to Journals in History, 1838--1974

several weaknesses. Some of its key word subject headings do not work effectively. For example, "education" gives you nine pages to wade through. Sometimes the titles of articles have been shortened so much that they turn out to be ambiguous or misleading. Of course, having only the beginning page is a nuisance, because you generally get more out of a long article than a short one, and *C.R.I.S.* does not tell which to pursue on that account.

The most useful specialized index for history undergraduates, one that is both a bibliography and an index, is *Writings on American History* (Washington, DC: The American Historical Association; Millwood, NY: KTO Press, 1904–). This has been issued by the American Historical Association since 1909 and until 1960 it was comprehensive; its goal was to list everything published in the relevant year. The slowness of publication was a great problem and by 1972, when the latest volume published was that for 1960, the editors decided to skip the gap and publish annual vol-

umes beginning with 1973/74. The twelve years from 1962 to 1973 were published in 1976 in a four-volume subject bibliography. However, these volumes are awkward to use because there is only an author index to the 33,000 articles which are listed under time periods (volume 1), geographical areas (volume 2), and subjects (volumes 3 and 4). The categories under which items are listed are so broad that it takes a long time to read through them.

When you are using *Writings on American History*, it helps to remember that the volumes before 1962 included books and journal articles, but after 1961 the annual volumes list articles only, some in foreign languages. With the 1973/74 volume some changes were made that will affect your research. The older volumes had a subject arrangement that divided the material into three main sections: the historical profession, national history, and regional, state, and local history. Beginning with 1973/74 there were also three sections, but they were named chronological, geographical, and

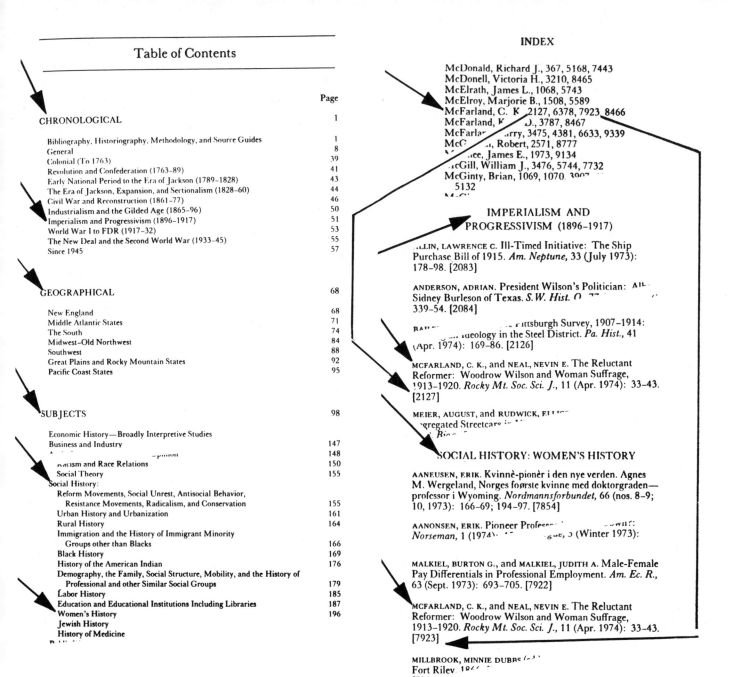

Table of Contents

INDEX

IMPERIALISM AND PROGRESSIVISM (1896–1917)

...LIN, LAWRENCE C. Ill-Timed Initiative: The Ship Purchase Bill of 1915. *Am. Neptune*, 33 (July 1973): 178–98. [2083]

ANDERSON, ADRIAN. President Wilson's Politician: A... Sidney Burleson of Texas. *S. W. Hist. Q* ... 339–54. [2084]

BA... Pittsburgh Survey, 1907–1914: ... ...ueology in the Steel District. *Pa. Hist.*, 41 (Apr. 1974): 169–86. [2126]

MCFARLAND, C. K., and NEAL, NEVIN E. The Reluctant Reformer: Woodrow Wilson and Woman Suffrage, 1913–1920. *Rocky Mt. Soc. Sci. J.*, 11 (Apr. 1974): 33–43. [2127]

MEIER, AUGUST, and RUDWICK, ELL... ...gregated Streetcars in ... ...*Bus* ...

SOCIAL HISTORY: WOMEN'S HISTORY

AANEUSEN, ERIK. Kvinnè-pionèr i den nye verden. Agnes M. Wergeland, Norges foørste kvinne med doktorgraden—professor i Wyoming. *Nordmannsforbundet*, 66 (nos. 8–9; 10, 1973): 166–69; 194–97. [7854]

AANONSEN, ERIK. Pioneer Profess... ...wn... *Norseman*, 1 (1974)... ...ue, 5 (Winter 1973):

MALKIEL, BURTON G., and MALKIEL, JUDITH A. Male-Female Pay Differentials in Professional Employment. *Am. Ec. R.*, 63 (Sept. 1973): 693–705. [7922]

MCFARLAND, C. K., and NEAL, NEVIN E. The Reluctant Reformer: Woodrow Wilson and Woman Suffrage, 1913–1920. *Rocky Mt. Soc. Sci. J.*, 11 (Apr. 1974): 33–43. [7923]

MILLBROOK, MINNIE DUBBS ... Fort Riley ... ...

FIGURE 26. Writings on American History

subjects, as shown in FIGURE 26. An article like McFarland and Neal "The Reluctant Reformer: Woodrow Wilson and Woman Suffrage, 1913–1920" in the *Rocky Mountain Social Science Journal* (vol. 11, April 1974, pp. 33–43) appears both in the chronological listing (1896–1917) and the subject listing (Social history: Women's history), as shown in FIGURE 26. Since there is no subject index, you can locate such an article only through the author index, shown in FIGURE 26, or the table of contents, also shown in FIGURE 26. In fact, the article is the same one that you located by using the *Social Sciences Citation Index*.

The newer volumes are made up by using the *American Historical Review*'s regular feature, "Recently Published Articles," plus other articles and dissertations. The list in the *AHR* is alphabetical by author. The *Writings on American History* supplies the subject approach and also includes an index to authors.

Abstracts

An abstracting service providing you with a brief summary of each article, can be of enormous aid when it comes to selecting for reading only those articles most focused on your topic. The foremost abstracting services for historians are *Historical Abstracts* (Santa Barbara, CA: ABC–CLIO,

1955–) which deals with history in all countries except the U.S. and Canada, and its off-shoot *America: History and Life.*

America: History and Life (Santa Barbara, CA: ABC-CLIO, 1964–) offers an abstracting index to close to 2200 serials from all over the world and in many languages. It presents articles on the history and culture of the United States and Canada. The abstracts are grouped into six broad sections: North America; Canada; United States of America, National History to 1945; United States of America, 1945 to Present; United States of America, Regional, State and Local History; and finally History, The Humanities, and Social Sciences. Each section is further subdivided. Such a classified arrangement seems an easy one until you realize that to find material on women's suffrage and the anti-suffrage movement one needs to go through an entire subsection covering American history between 1877 and 1917. It has a detailed subject index using four or five subject index terms for each article, plus some geographical index terms and the dates that the article covers. A portion of this index from the 1976 volume is shown in FIGURE 27. In the marked entry you can see that the article refers to women's suffrage, to the American Antislavery Society, to Susan B. Anthony, and to the 19th Amendment to the Constitution. You can also see that it covers the 1840's to 1920. The final number, 13A:473, tells you that the abstract is number 473 in the thirteenth volume, part A, of *America: History and Life.* This detailed subject index began in Volume 11. Earlier, searches for articles on women's suffrage in the index yielded only broad subjects like "Women" and made searching tedious. The newer issues include a Part A, abstracts of journal articles; a Part B, index to book reviews; a Part C, a bibliography (with no abstracts) of books, articles and dissertations; and a Part D, an annual subject index (a sample of which you have seen in FIGURE 27). If you do find an abstract of an article you want, you will find that *America: History and Life* very helpfully tells you exactly what kind of documentation (diaries, letters, etc.) the research is based upon.

Writing a paper in history often entails using specialized indexes and abstracts outside the field of history. For example, when doing an historical paper on women's suffrage, in addition to historical sources, you will want to exploit the women's sources available. An excellent abstracting service in the field of women's studies is *Women Studies Abstracts* (Rush, NY: Rush, 1972–) which regularly scans both popular and scholarly periodicals and research papers for material on women, abstracting most, listing others. They are arranged by broad subject area (the area you will find most pertinent being "History") with a detailed subject index. FIGURE 28 shows a sample of an abstract on the topic of the antisuffrage movement, giving you all the bibliographic information you want plus a brief outline of the article.

Newspaper Indexes

For a contemporary, exciting view of events, nothing beats newspapers. Local newspapers are often difficult to get into as they may not be indexed. But, as you have already discovered (in Chapter 6), an excellent index is available for the *New York Times.* This can be used for current articles

SUBJECT INDEX

Woman suffrage. American Antislavery Society. Anthony, Susan B. Constitutional Amendments (19th). 1840's-1920. *13A:473*
—. British North America Act of 1929. Canada. 1870's-1940's. *13A:2868 13C:619*
—. Catt, Carrie Chapman. Duniway, Abigail Scott. Idaho., National American Woman Suffrage Association. Women's Christian Temperance Union. 1870-96. *13A:2564*
—. Constitutional Amendments (19th). Feminists. Pennsylvania. 1837-1920. *13A:2027*
—. Constitutions, State. Duniway, Abigail Scott. Oregon. Voting rights. 1860's-1912. *13A:7049 13C:6909*
—. Martin, Anne. Nevada. 1869-1914. *13C:6905*
—. Methodist Protestant Church. Shaw, Anna Howard. Social Gospel Movement. 1880-1919. *13A:3283 13C:2310*
—. Mormon Church. Utah. 1895. *13A:7075 13C:6952*
—. National Association of Colored Women. Negroes. Reform and Reformers. Terrell, Mary Church. 1892-1954. *13A:5022 13C:1020*
—. Religious Issues. 19c. *13C:949*
Woman suffrage campaigns. Colorado.

ARTICLE ABSTRACTS AND CITATIONS

13A:473. Robbins, Peggy. SUSAN B. ANTHONY. *Am. Hist. Illus. 1971 6(5): 36-43.* Susan Brownell Anthony (1820-1906) was born in Adams, Massachusetts, of Quaker parents. In the late 1840's, she became active in temperance, antislavery movements, and women's rights, devoting her full time after 1849 to "social action." Although the years 1855-65 were devoted to the American Antislavery Society in New York, Susan also led the fight which resulted in an 1860 New York law granting property rights to married women. After the Civil War, she concentrated on winning woman suffrage, and 14 years after she died the 19th Amendment was ratified, 26 August 1920, often called the "Susan Anthony Amendment." Secondary sources; 5 illus. D. Dodd

13A:474. Rodino, Peter. TODAY'S NEED FOR IMMIGRATION REVISION. *Internat. Migration R. 1970 4(3): 11-15.* Reviews the history of US immigration policy and contends that it has been a series of emergency reactions to specific circumstances. A mature immigration policy is needed like the one embodied in HR17370, sponsored by Congressman Peter Rodino. This bill creates a world-wide ceiling on immigration, an amenable refugee system, a proper preference system, and eliminates accumulations of brothers and sisters awaiting visas. G. O. Gagnon

FIGURE 27. America: History and Life

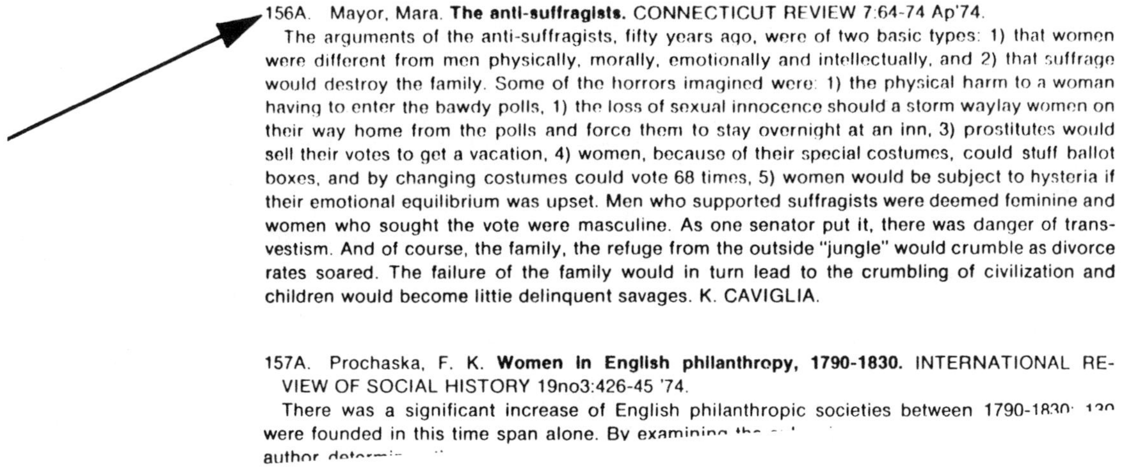

156A. Mayor, Mara. **The anti-suffragists.** CONNECTICUT REVIEW 7:64-74 Ap'74.

The arguments of the anti-suffragists, fifty years ago, were of two basic types: 1) that women were different from men physically, morally, emotionally and intellectually, and 2) that suffrage would destroy the family. Some of the horrors imagined were: 1) the physical harm to a woman having to enter the bawdy polls, 1) the loss of sexual innocence should a storm waylay women on their way home from the polls and force them to stay overnight at an inn, 3) prostitutes would sell their votes to get a vacation, 4) women, because of their special costumes, could stuff ballot boxes, and by changing costumes could vote 68 times, 5) women would be subject to hysteria if their emotional equilibrium was upset. Men who supported suffragists were deemed feminine and women who sought the vote were masculine. As one senator put it, there was danger of trans-vestism. And of course, the family, the refuge from the outside "jungle" would crumble as divorce rates soared. The failure of the family would in turn lead to the crumbling of civilization and children would become little delinquent savages. K. CAVIGLIA.

157A. Prochaska, F. K. **Women in English philanthropy, 1790-1830.** INTERNATIONAL RE-VIEW OF SOCIAL HISTORY 19no3:426-45 '74.

There was a significant increase of English philanthropic societies between 1790-1830. 120 were founded in this time span alone. By examining the ～′
author deter～

FIGURE 28. Women's Studies Abstracts

on recent developments of the women's movement which have historical antecedents, as well as for articles from the suffrage period and for biography. Keep in mind, for instance, that the magazine section of the Sunday *New York Times* could run an article comparing the organization behind the suffrage movement with that behind the Equal Rights Amendment. Remember too that the dates of events found through the *New York Times Index* can be used to look at articles on the same events which appear in other newspapers.

Summary

1. You need current information for current topics and to find the latest research on older topics. You will find some of this information through the latest bibliographies you have already looked at, and even more through periodical indexes and abstracting services.

2. Go first to the general indexes, especially *Humanities Index*, which covers the most important scholarly history periodicals.

3. Use the citation approach available through *Social Sciences Citation Index*.

4. Search carefully in comprehensive historical indexes, like *Writings on American History*.

5. Examine pertinent abstracting services.

6. Check newspaper indexes for contemporary accounts of events as they occurred.

History, in general, only informs us what bad government is.

Thomas Jefferson. *Writings.*

If you are like the majority of library users, researchers, and students, you will ask, "Can't I avoid government documents? I've always heard they are hard to use." Actually, there is a tremendous wealth of material in documents, a rich lode of data and opinion, that you can learn to mine. Documents also provide official, accurate wording for pronouncements that made or influenced history. Sometimes they provide discussion pro and con on controversial issues. So the answer to, "Can't I avoid government documents?" has to be, for the sake of perspective, information, and documentation, "No."

Contrary to popular belief, documents are not necessarily difficult to find once you understand the primary bibliographic tools that give access to them.

The *Monthly Catalog of United States Government Documents* and its predecessors provide the basic index to the documents of the legislative and executive branches of government. The *Congressional Record* and its predecessors are the record of actions in Congress, particularly of the debates and sessions on the floor of both houses. The Serial Set, whose contents have varied through the years, contains some of the most basic documents of committee work.

Using these you can trace, for instance, arguments pro and con the passing of legislation giving women the vote, perhaps getting some documentary evidence of the interests that lay behind the opposition.

One clarification here: in the paragraphs above, the word "documents" and "documentation" have been used with two meanings. Ordinarily, in history research a document is any written material being examined as primary evidence in an argument. For example, a written speech is a document and a diary may be used as documentary evidence of a personal viewpoint on an issue. In this sense we use "documents" meaning "historical documents." On the other hand we also use the term "documents" to describe any published material issuing from the government. In this sense we use "documents" to mean "government documents." To make it more complex "government documents" can be "historical documents," and vice versa. We shall try to keep the distinctions clear, particularly in this chapter on government documents. Let's look at each title in turn.

Using the *Monthly Catalog*

The *Monthly Catalog of United States Government Publications* (Washington, DC: Government Printing Office, 1895 to date) has had a number of name changes since it began in the 19th century. It is issued monthly and lists, by issuing agency, (see FIGURE 29B), most government publications sent through the Government Printing Office.

In FIGURE 29A you see a sample of the 1918 index to authors, agencies, titles, and subjects. When you locate the item you want, you will notice a page number beside it. In

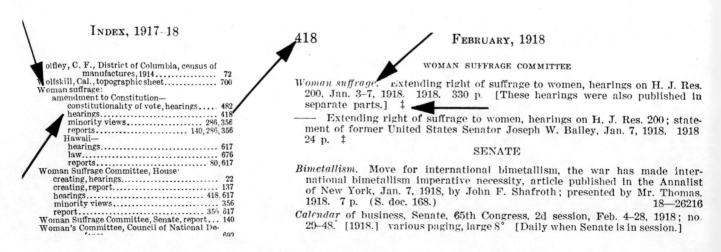

FIGURE 29A. Monthly Catalogue of United States Public Documents

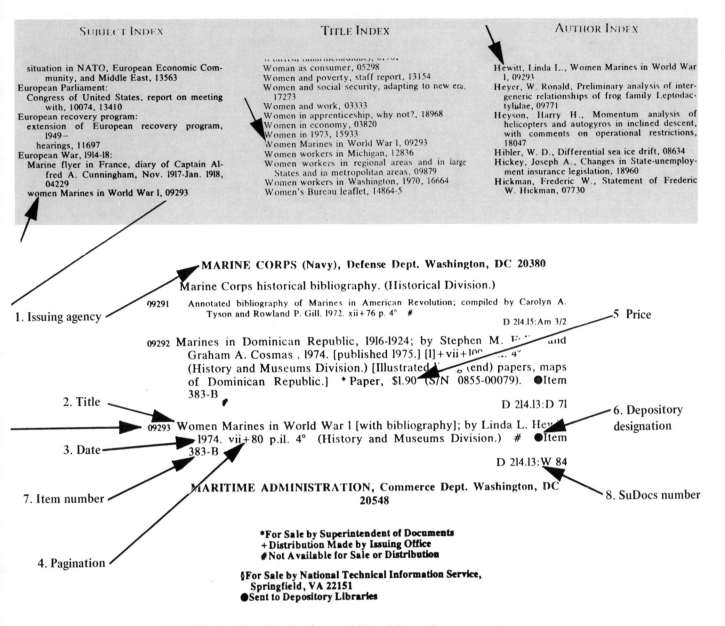

MARINE CORPS (Navy), Defense Dept. Washington, DC 20380

Marine Corps historical bibliography. (Historical Division.)

09291   Annotated bibliography of Marines in American Revolution; compiled by Carolyn A. Tyson and Rowland P. Gill. 1972. xii+76 p. 4° #

D 214.15:Am 3/2

09292 Marines in Dominican Republic, 1916-1924; by Stephen M. F... and Graham A. Cosmas . 1974. [published 1975.] [I]+vii+10... .. 4° (History and Museums Division.) [Illustrated... (end) papers, maps of Dominican Republic.] * Paper, $1.90 (S/N 0855-00079). ●Item 383-B

D 214.13:D 71

09293 Women Marines in World War I [with bibliography]; by Linda L. Hey... 1974. vii+80 p.il. 4° (History and Museums Division.) # ●Item 383-B

D 214.13:W 84

MARITIME ADMINISTRATION, Commerce Dept. Washington, DC 20548

1. Issuing agency
2. Title
3. Date
7. Item number
4. Pagination
5. Price
6. Depository designation
8. SuDocs number

*For Sale by Superintendent of Documents
+ Distribution Made by Issuing Office
# Not Available for Sale or Distribution

§For Sale by National Technical Information Service, Springfield, VA 22151
●Sent to Depository Libraries

FIGURE 29B. Monthly Catalogue of United States Government Documents

the example in FIGURE 29A the page number is 418. In 1947 this number ceased to be a page number and became an entry number instead, referring directly to the desired publication.

The index to the *Monthly Catalog* should be approached with some caution. Subjects are not cross–referenced as completely as they could be; occasionally you will have to try several possible approaches. Furthermore, in 1974 the index was split into three parts: where before 1974 the index was one interfiled author/agency/title/subject index, after that date there is one subject index, one author index and one title index. See FIGURE 29B for an illustration of the three separate indexes and their entries for one item. Take care that you are using the correct index for what you need.

Once you have found the entry numbers for material you want, you can turn to the body of the listing and there you will find your item described. FIGURE 29A shows the listing for the entry we located through the index mentioned above. Notice the information supplied. The issuing agency stands at the head of the listing, then the title, date, and pagination. The tiny double dagger indicates that this item was not available for distribution. It is one of the more interesting facts about the many hearings that were held at the time on women's suffrage, that none of the documents were distributed.

Compare this entry with more recent ones, as shown in FIGURE 29B, entries in the 1975 *Monthly Catalog*, one of which is for the item you found indexed in FIGURE 29B, which again shows the issuing agency (Marine Corps), the title, date of publication, and pagination, but usually adds the price, item number and the apparently complex Superintendent of Documents number. The cost figure is easy to

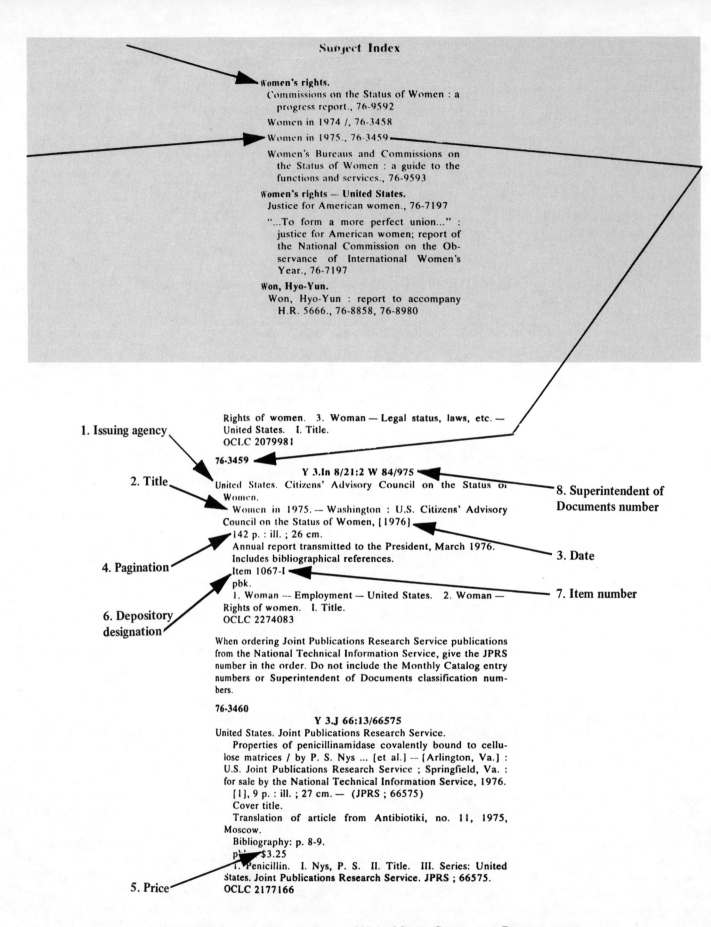

Women's rights.
Commissions on the Status of Women : a progress report., 76-9592

Women in 1974 /, 76-3458

Women in 1975., 76-3459

Women's Bureaus and Commissions on the Status of Women : a guide to the functions and services., 76-9593

Women's rights — United States.
Justice for American women., 76-7197

"...To form a more perfect union..." : justice for American women; report of the National Commission on the Observance of International Women's Year., 76-7197

Won, Hyo-Yun.
Won, Hyo-Yun : report to accompany H.R. 5666., 76-8858, 76-8980

---

1. Issuing agency

2. Title

4. Pagination

6. Depository designation

Rights of women. 3. Woman — Legal status, laws, etc. — United States. I. Title.
OCLC 2079981

76-3459

Y 3.In 8/21:2 W 84/975

United States. Citizens' Advisory Council on the Status of Women.

Women in 1975. — Washington : U.S. Citizens' Advisory Council on the Status of Women, [1976]

142 p. : ill. ; 26 cm.
Annual report transmitted to the President, March 1976.
Includes bibliographical references.

Item 1067-I
pbk.

1. Woman — Employment — United States. 2. Woman — Rights of women. I. Title.
OCLC 2274083

8. Superintendent of Documents number

3. Date

7. Item number

When ordering Joint Publications Research Service publications from the National Technical Information Service, give the JPRS number in the order. Do not include the Monthly Catalog entry numbers or Superintendent of Documents classification numbers.

76-3460

Y 3.J 66:13/66575

United States. Joint Publications Research Service.

Properties of penicillinamidase covalently bound to cellulose matrices / by P. S. Nys ... [et al.] — [Arlington, Va.] : U.S. Joint Publications Research Service ; Springfield, Va. : for sale by the National Technical Information Service, 1976.

[1], 9 p. : ill. ; 27 cm. — (JPRS ; 66575)
Cover title.
Translation of article from Antibiotiki, no. 11, 1975, Moscow.
Bibliography: p. 8-9.
pbk. $3.25
1. Penicillin. I. Nys, P. S. II. Title. III. Series: United States. Joint Publications Research Service. JPRS ; 66575.
OCLC 2177166

5. Price

FIGURE 29C. Monthly Catalogue of United States Government Documents

understand. But what is the item number? And what is the large dot beside it? The item number indicates a category of documents and need not concern you. But the dot beside the number – decoded at the bottom of the page – indicates that this is an item available free to depository libraries and, if your library has been designated a depository or selective depository, it is likely to have that document.

In July 1976 the *Monthly Catalog* underwent further revision. While the revision did not alter the catalog substantially, it did make a noticeable difference in format. You have only to look at the new index and at the sample entry in FIGURE 29C, both from the 1976 *Monthly Catalog*, to see the change. The index section still includes an author, a title and a subject index. The differences are that it adds a report number index and that it now uses subjects from the *Library of Congress Subject Headings* that you grappled with in Chapter 4. This use of the subject headings from LC makes it simpler for you to move from locating books on your topic in the card catalog, to locating documents in the *Monthly Catalog*. Using the same subject that you used in the card catalog, search the subject index at the back of the *Monthly Catalog*. When you locate an item there that you want, note the entry number. Use the entry number to locate the item in the body of the catalog. There you can note both the information given about the item (its bibliographic citation and the subjects assigned to it) and its Superintendent of Documents number, before going to the shelf for the item itself.

The Superintendent of Documents number places the document in a classification scheme that was begun at the turn of the century and appears in the *Monthly Catalog* for the first time in 1924. Look again at FIGURE 29B, and notice the Superintendent of Documents number given to entry 09293 (D 214.13:W 84). That number is constructed to show the document's origin and its nature. In this example each section of the number breaks down as follows:

D	Defense Department
214:	Marine Corps
13:	Historical Publications
W 84	Book number, here using 'W' for the key word in the title.

If the documents in your library are shelved by this Superintendent of Documents number, you will have the advantage of finding similar documents from the same agency shelved close to it. Some libraries give each document a number which shelves it with the other books in the regular collection. In that case you need to search the card catalog for your document.

To summarize the benefits of the *Monthly Catalog*, it provides you with an index to legislative and executive document of the United States government.

Using the *Document Catalogue*

There is one catalog of government documents that overlaps the *Monthly Catalog*. For the years it covers, how-

ever, the *Catalogue of the Public Documents of the . . . Congress and of all Departments of the Government of the United States . . .* (Washington, DC: Government Printing Office, 1896–1945), familiarly known as the *Document Catalogue*, gives more complete coverage than the *Monthly Catalog*. The *Document Catalogue* covers the years 1893 to 1940 and lists publications of the government with entries under personal author, agency author, subject and even title. The information given about each entry is substantial,

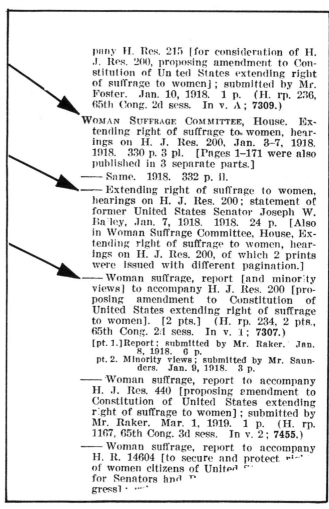

FIGURE 30
Catalogue of the Public Documents
of the 65th Congress

as you can see from FIGURE 30, which shows the entry for the same item that you located through the *Monthly Catalogue*. The *Document Catalogue* is an example of a beautifully crafted index. It was never intended to be a current index or a sales list. That was to be the function of the *Monthly Catalogue*. However, as that latter publication improved, publication of the *Document Catalogue* was more and more of a luxury and was finally dropped. For the years between 1893 and 1940, however, the *Document Catalogue* offers the best access to government publications.

BILL INTRODUCED

251

BILLS INTRODUCED.

Mr. BAILEY asked, and by unanimous consent obtained, leave to introduce a bill (S. No. 475) for the relief of William L. Nance; which was read twice by its title, and referred to the Committee on Claims.

Mr. SARGENT asked, and by unanimous consent obtained, leave to introduce a bill (S. No. 476) to relieve certain legal disabilities of women; which was read twice by its title, and referred to the Committee on the Judiciary.

He also asked, and by unanimous consent obtained, leave to introduce a bill (S. No. 477) to regulate Chinese immigration; which was read twice by its title.

Mr. SARGENT. I should like to have the bill referred to the Committee on Foreign Relations, and I wish to make one remark in reference to it. The bill was introduced in the House of Represent-atives originally by Mr. SHELLEY, of Alabama. I_ ject of very great importance _. C __ coast, and I b__

BILL DEBATED

WOMAN SUFFRAGE.

Mr. BLAIR. I now move that the Senate proceed to consider the joint resolution (S. R. 5) proposing an amendment to the Constitution of the United States extending the right of suffrage to women.

The motion was agreed to; and the Senate, as in Committee of the Whole, proceeded to consider the joint resolution.

The PRESIDING OFFICER. The joint resolution will be read.

The Chief Clerk read the joint resolution, as follows:

Resolved (two-thirds of each House concurring therein), That the following article be proposed to the Legislatures of the several States as an amendment to the Constitution of the United States; which, when ratified by three-fourths of the said Legislatures, shall be valid as part of said Constitution, namely:

ARTICLE —.

SECTION 1. The right of citizens of the United States to vote shall not be denied or abridged by the United States or by any State on account of sex.

SEC. 2. The Congress shall have power, by appropriate legislation, to enforce the provisions of this article.

Mr. BROWN. Mr. President, the joint resolution introduced by my friend, the Senator from New Hampshire [Mr. BLAIR], proposing an amendment to the Constitution of the United States, conferring the right to vote upon the women of the United States, is one of paramount importance, as it involves great questions far reaching in their tendency, which seriously affect the very pillars of our social fabric, which involve the peace and harmony of society, the unity of the family, and much of the future success of our Government. The question should therefore be met fairly and discussed with firmness, but with moderation and forbearance.

No one contributes anything valuable to the debate by the use of harsh terms, or by impugning motives, or by disparaging the arguments of the opposition. Where the prosperity of the race and the peace of society are involved, we should, on both sides, meet fairly the arguments of our respective opponents.

This question has been discussed _ _ ____

ioned type of womanhood, the wife and the mother.

And the result of the woman movement seems more or less in a line thus far with this theoretic aim. Of advanced women a less proportion are inclined to marry than of the old-fashioned type; of those who do marry a great proportion are restless in marriage bonds or seek release from them, while of those who do remain in married life many bear no children, and few, indeed, become mothers of large families. The woman's vitality is concentrated in the brain and fructifies more in intellectual than in physical forms.

Now, women who do not marry are one of two things; either they belong to a class which we shrink from naming or they become old maids.

An old maid may be in herself a very useful and commendable person and a valuable member of society; many are all this. But she has still this sad drawback, she can not perpetuate herself; and since all history and observation go to prove that the great final end of creation, whatever it may be, can only be achieved through the perpetuity and increasing progress of the race, it follows that unmarried woman is not the most necessary, the indispensable type of woman. If there were no other class of females left upon the earth but the women who do not bear children, then the world would be a failure, creation would be unplussed.

If, then, the movement for the emancipation of woman has for its final end the making of never so fine a quality, never so sublimated a sort of non-child-bearing women, it is an absurdity upon the face of it.

From the standpoint of the Chimney Corner it appears that too many even of the most gifted and liberal-minded of the leaders in th_ rights movement have not __ __

BILL PASSED

MESSAGE FROM THE HOUSE.

A message from the House of Representatives, by D. K. Hempstead, its enrolling clerk, announced that the House had passed a bill (H. R. 3157) making appropriations for the Department of Agriculture for the fiscal year ending June 30, 1920, in which it requested the concurrence of the Senate.

ENROLLED JOINT RESOLUTION SIGNED.

The message also announced that the Speaker of the House had signed the enrolled joint resolution (H. J. Res. 1) proposing an amendment to the Constitution extending the right of suffrage to women, and it was thereupon signed by the Vice President.

HISTORY OF BILLS

HOUSE JOINT RESOLUTIONS

FIGURE 31. Congressional Record

Using the *Congressional Record*

Debates on the floor of Congress provide some insight into contemporary views on such issues as suffrage. The *Congressional Record* . . . (Washington, DC: Government Printing Office, 1873 to date) and its predecessors, *Annals of Congress* . . . (1789 to 1824), *Register of Debates* . . . (1824 to 1837), and *Congressional Globe* . . . (1833 to 1873), are the records of these debates, although the right of members to add to, to alter, or delete from the verbatim account, keeps the *Record* from being a strict account of the proceedings.

The *Congressional Record* can also aid you in tracing the history of a bill through Congress. FIGURE 31 shows the general index to the *Congressional Record* for the 45th Congress in 1878, directing the user to page 251 of the *Record* where you can see the printed record of the first introduction of Susan B. Anthony's suffrage bill on January 10, 1878, by the Hon. A.A. Sargent. It is a peaceful enough introduction. The debate, a small portion of which you see in FIGURE 31, was longer than what is shown here. Notice of the bill's final passage is recorded, fifty–nine years later, in the 1919 *Record* as shown (again in FIGURE 31), in as terse a fashion as its introduction.

FIGURE 31 shows another aspect of the *Congressional Record*. This section traces the history of bills and refers you to sections of the *Record*. Look, for instance, at H.J. Res. 1 which, as you have just seen, eventually achieved passage.

Using the Serial Set

The Serial Set (Washington, DC: Government Printing Office, 1789–), sometimes called the Congressional Series, provides another key to congressional action. While the *Congressional Record* contains debates, and while the hearings supply testimony given before committees, the Serial Set includes the documents which congressional committees produce in the course of their investigations, and the reports they send back to Congress. An example of such a report – the report to Congress from the Committee on Woman Suffrage of the House of Representatives, 1919-- is shown in FIGURE 32. Basically, then, the Serial Set contains four types of publications: House Documents (H. doc.), House Reports (H. rp.), Senate Documents (S. doc.), and Senate Reports (S. rp.). The set also contains annual reports and proceedings of some few particular organizations such as the American Legion, Daughters of the American Revolution, Boy Scouts of America and Girl Scouts of the U.S.A.

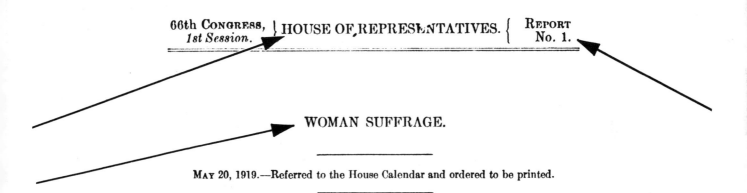

66th Congress,
1st Session.   HOUSE OF REPRESENTATIVES.   Report No. 1.

WOMAN SUFFRAGE.

May 20, 1919.—Referred to the House Calendar and ordered to be printed.

Mr. Mann, from the Committee on Woman Suffrage, submitted the following

REPORT.

[To accompany H. J. Res. No. 1.]

The Committee on Woman Suffrage, to which was referred the resolution (H. J. Res. 1) proposing an amendment to the Constitution extending the right of suffrage to women, after consideration, report the said resolution back to the House with a recommendation that it do pass.

FIGURE 32. Congress. House. *Woman Suffrage*

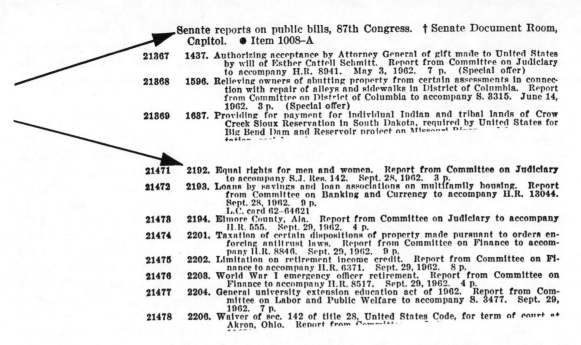

21367 1437. Authorizing acceptance by Attorney General of gift made to United States by will of Esther Cattell Schmitt. Report from Committee on Judiciary to accompany H.R. 8941. May 3, 1962. 7 p. (Special offer)

21368 1596. Relieving owners of abutting property from certain assessments in connection with repair of alleys and sidewalks in District of Columbia. Report from Committee on District of Columbia to accompany S. 3315. June 14, 1962. 3 p. (Special offer)

21369 1637. Providing for payment for individual Indian and tribal lands of Crow Creek Sioux Reservation in South Dakota, required by United States for Big Bend Dam and Reservoir project on Missouri River...

21471 2102. Equal rights for men and women. Report from Committee on Judiciary to accompany S.J. Res. 142. Sept. 28, 1962. 3 p.

21472 2193. Loans by savings and loan associations on multifamily housing. Report from Committee on Banking and Currency to accompany H.R. 13044. Sept. 28, 1962. 9 p. L.C. card 62-64621

21473 2194. Elmore County, Ala. Report from Committee on Judiciary to accompany H.R. 555. Sept. 29, 1962. 4 p.

21474 2201. Taxation of certain dispositions of property made pursuant to orders enforcing antitrust laws. Report from Committee on Finance to accompany H.R. 8846. Sept. 29, 1962. 9 p.

21475 2202. Limitation on retirement income credit. Report from Committee on Finance to accompany H.R. 6371. Sept. 29, 1962. 8 p.

21476 2203. World War I emergency officer retirement. Report from Committee on Finance to accompany H.R. 8517. Sept. 29, 1962. 4 p.

21477 2204. General university extension education act of 1962. Report from Committee on Labor and Public Welfare to accompany S. 3477. Sept. 29, 1962. 7 p.

21478 2206. Waiver of sec. 142 of title 28, United States Code, for term of court at Akron, Ohio. Report from Committee...

FIGURE 33. Monthly Catalog of United States Government Publications

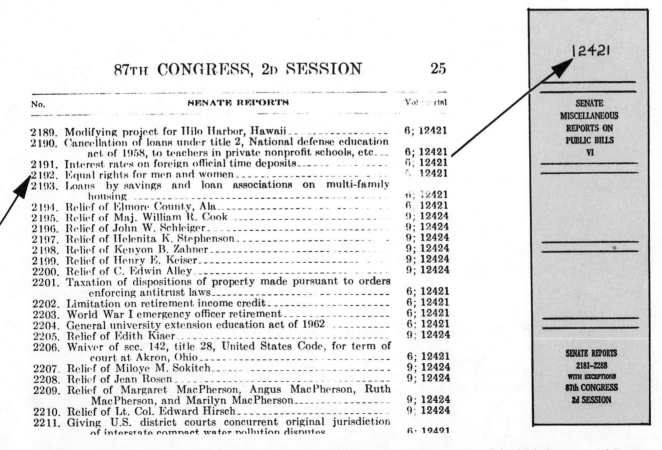

87TH CONGRESS, 2D SESSION — 25

No.	SENATE REPORTS	Vol.; serial
2189.	Modifying project for Hilo Harbor, Hawaii	6; 12421
2190.	Cancellation of loans under title 2, National defense education act of 1958, to teachers in private nonprofit schools, etc.	6; 12421
2191.	Interest rates on foreign official time deposits	6; 12421
2192.	Equal rights for men and women	6; 12421
2193.	Loans by savings and loan associations on multi-family housing	6; 12421
2194.	Relief of Elmore County, Ala	6; 12421
2195.	Relief of Maj. William R. Cook	9; 12424
2196.	Relief of John W. Schleiger	9; 12424
2197.	Relief of Helenita K. Stephenson	9; 12424
2198.	Relief of Kenyon B. Zahner	9; 12424
2199.	Relief of Henry E. Keiser	9; 12424
2200.	Relief of C. Edwin Alley	9; 12424
2201.	Taxation of dispositions of property made pursuant to orders enforcing antitrust laws	6; 12421
2202.	Limitation on retirement income credit	6; 12421
2203.	World War I emergency officer retirement	6; 12421
2204.	General university extension education act of 1962	6; 12421
2205.	Relief of Edith Kiaer	9; 12424
2206.	Waiver of sec. 142, title 28, United States Code, for term of court at Akron, Ohio	6; 12421
2207.	Relief of Miloye M. Sokitch	9; 12424
2208.	Relief of Jean Rosen	9; 12424
2209.	Relief of Margaret MacPherson, Angus MacPherson, Ruth MacPherson, and Marilyn MacPherson	9; 12424
2210.	Relief of Lt. Col. Edward Hirsch	9; 12424
2211.	Giving U.S. district courts concurrent original jurisdiction of interstate compact water pollution disputes	6; 12421

12421

SENATE MISCELLANEOUS REPORTS ON PUBLIC BILLS VI

SENATE REPORTS 2181-2288 WITH EXCEPTIONS 87th CONGRESS 2d SESSION

FIGURE 34. Numerical Lists and Schedule of Volumes of the Reports and Documents of the 87th Congress, 2d Session

The House and Senate Manuals and the Constitution are also here, among other documents. For the most part you will be interested in the House and Senate Documents and Reports. When these papers are bound into permanent volumes they may be thrown out of numerical order, so users need an indication of the volume in which each document or report appears. FIGURE 30 illustrates that the *Document Catalogue* gives this information. For example, House Report 234 of the 65th Congress appears in Serial Set volume number 7307. The *Monthly Catalog* listing of these documents and reports appears before they are bound into the permanent volumes and consequently cannot give this helpful information. So in order to find the correct volume for the report shown in FIGURE 33, you must use the *Numerical Lists and Schedule of Volumes* (Washington, DC: Government Printing Office, 1942 to date). The number of the report found in FIGURE 33 is S. Rp. 87–2192 indicating the Congress and the report number. (Note that the entry, or marginal, number is 21471 and no Superintendent of Documents number is assigned.) To find what volume of the Serial Set this report is in, look at the *Numerical Lists*, as illustrated in FIGURE 34, where you are told that this page is the listing for the 87th Congress, Senate Reports. Down the left side are the numbers of each report. Yours is 2192. Following that number you find the title of the report and then the Serial Set number – 12421. On the shelf the volume itself will look like FIGURE 34, and the report itself begins as appears in FIGURE 35.

Guides to Government Documents

More extensive guidance to government documents is available from two books which are probably in your library. The first is Laurance F. Schmeckebier and Roy B. Eastin, *Government Publications and Their Use*, 2d ed., (Washington, DC: Brookings Institution, 1969) which gives a thorough description, including detailed historical information, about documents. The second gives less historical information, but is an easier account to follow and is more up-to-date. It is Joe Morehead's *Introduction to United States Public Documents*, 2d ed., (Littleton, CO: Libraries Unlimited, 1978).

Documents are sometimes complicated. Don't hesitate to ask a librarian for assistance in using them.

Summary

1. Government documents are a rich source of material. Learn the basic methods for finding them and practice locating the items you need.
2. Use the *Monthly Catalog of United States Government Documents* to locate legislative and executive documents. Go from the index to the entry in the *Monthly Catalog* to find issuing agent, title, date, and Superintendent of Documents number of the item you want.

Calendar No. 2155

| 87TH CONGRESS 2d Session | SENATE | REPORT No. 2192 |

EQUAL RIGHTS FOR MEN AND WOMEN

SEPTEMBER 28, 1962.—Ordered to be printed

Mr. EASTLAND, from the Committee on the Judiciary, submitted the following

REPORT

[To accompany S.J. Res. 142]

The Committee on the Judiciary, to which was referred the joint resolution (S.J. Res. 142) proposing an amendment to the Constitution of the United States concerning equal rights under law for men and women, having considered the same, reports favorably thereon, without amendment, and recommends that the joint resolution do pass.

PURPOSE

The purpose of the proposed joint resolution is to submit to the State legislatures an amendment to the Constitution of the United States which, if adopted, would insure equal rights under the law for men and women.

STATEMENT

The substantive section of the proposed amendment is quite simple and straightforward. It reads as follows:

Equality of rights under the law shall not be denied or abridged by the United States or by any State on account of sex. Congress and the several States shall have power, within their respective jurisdictions, to enforce this article by appropriate legislation.

Senate Joint Resolution 142 was introduced in the 87th Congress by Senator McGee for himself and 34 other Senators as cosponsors. Identical resolutions have been introduced in the House of Representatives by 136 Members. During this Congress, the Legislatures

85006

FIGURE 35
U.S. Congress. Senate.
Equal Rights for Men and Women

---

3. Use the *Document Catalogue* for a more detailed listing of those documents published between 1893 and 1940.
4. Use the *Congressional Record* and its predecessors to find the debates and proceedings of Congress.
5. In addition, use the *Congressional Record* to trace the history of bills once you know a bill number.
6. The Serial Set brings together House and Senate documents, which are materials requested by the committees to aid in their deliberations, and the House and Senate Reports, which are the committees' recommendations on the bills they send to Congress.
7. For further help consult your reference librarian and guides to government documents.

History is the essence of
innumerable biographies.
Carlyle, *Essays: On History*

You have already searched for biographical information in looking at authors in Chapter 6. Many of the same sources are useful in seeking material on historical characters, and in such cases the same search methods can be used. *Biography Index*, as seen in FIGURE 21, is again the place to find listings of biography when those biographies appear in books, articles or collections. The *Dictionary of American Biography* is the reliable, scholarly source of United States biography, complete with a useful bibliography, including obituaries. And its counterpart, *Notable American Women* can similarly be culled for bibliography and sources. The *National Cyclopaedia of American Biography* is a comprehensive, though less careful, source of information. The *New York Times Index* is again an invaluable hunting ground for news stories, biography and obituary. FIGURE 22, for instance, shows the *NYTI* listing of the obituary notice for Elizabeth Cady Stanton. Even in this early year, 1902, the notation is similar to that in current issues, giving date, page, and column. *Who Was Who in America*, which goes back to 1607, is a source to use for brief facts about a figure's life.

In addition to these titles for historical material, there are at least three other sources you should look at. The first is the *Dictionary of National Biography* which we mentioned as the original model for the *Dictionary of American Biography*. Remember that many of the personalities connected with American history were, or remained, British and don't overlook the *DNB* as a resource.

The second source of which you should be aware is the encyclopedias. Remember the example in FIGURE 1 where the author of the *Americana* article specifically reminded you to see the separate biographies of suffragist leaders? The *Dictionary of American History*, on the other hand, carries no biographical articles, though you could, by using the index volume, find some pieces of information buried in articles.

Don't neglect the card catalog for biography. Subject cards under your figure's name will reveal both biography and autobiography.

Summary

1. Biography is a major source of material for the historian. Make yourself familiar with the prime sources for such material.
2. Check bibliographies of biography like *Biography Index*. The card catalog, as well as being an index to the library's holdings, is also a bibliography of the book-length biographies in the library.
3. Check biographical reference sources like the *Dictionary of American Biography*. Use the information you find there and follow up on the bibliographies they may provide.

To be ignorant of what happened before you were born is to be ever a child. For what is man's lifetime unless the memory of past events is woven with those of earlier times?
Cicero, Orator

The serious student of history will want to know the basic sources in the discipline. A guide to the literature satisfies this need. There are two kinds of such guides. The first kind tells you something about the discipline, about its component parts, about how research is done using certain reference sources. The second kind simply lists the best books in the field of history. It is a bibliography of major works in, for instance, American history.

This guide you are presently using is of the first sort. It lists the most basic reference sources and outlines a search strategy for a research paper, one you can apply to any of the papers you write in history. There are others. The most venerable is Wood Gray's *Historian's Handbook*, 2d ed. (Boston: Houghton Mifflin, 1964). He includes chapters on note-taking and elements of style for your paper. A central section is the "Pursuit of Evidence," a bibliography of reference sources published before the mid-1960's. F.N. McCoy wrote the excellent, compact *Researching and Writing in History* (Berkeley, CA: University of California Press, 1974) for the college student and structures his book around the step-by-step task (using a 12-weeks-of-work model!) of writing a research paper. It is particularly for students of English history. The broadest scope is covered in *Sources of Information in the Social Sciences* by Carl M. White, 2d ed. (Chicago: American Library Association, 1973). Its chapter, "History," outlines the discipline, lists basic works, and describes a selected list of reference sources. The six pages on American history include the section on progressivism shown in FIGURE 36.

A work that straddles our two categories of guides to the literature is Helen Poulton's thorough *The Historian's Handbook* (Norman, OK: University of Oklahoma Press, 1972). One chapter describes how to use the library and its catalogs, while each subsequent chapter is a bibliographic essay on the reference resources available to the serious history student. Every form of source, from dissertations to dictionaries, from government documents to guides to history, is described.

The second type of guide, the bibliography of basic sources in the literature, you have already encountered in the *Harvard Guide*. Other such sources are Henry Putney Beers' *Bibliographies in American History*, rev. ed. (New York: H.W. Wilson, 1942) and the grandmother of all guides to American history, A.B. Hart and Edward Channing's *Guide to the Study of American History* (Boston: Ginn, 1897), which was revised in 1912. Two that came a little later were the classic George M. Dutcher and others *Guide to Historical*

Literature (New York: Macmillan, 1931), which was later revised to become the currently valuable American Historical Association's *Guide to Historical Literature* (New York: Macmillan, 1961). Other guides shade down into straight bibliography.

Use guides that suit your purpose. If you want help with writing a paper that is carefully researched in an orderly fashion, or if you want to be able to reach for your guide and

---

PROGRESSIVISM

The great industrial growth and its style—the creation of huge, often uncontrolled corporations—brought forth a reaction centered in the Midwest. Progressives sought regulation of the nation's major industries and reform of governmental institutions that had failed to protect the weak from the economically strong. Three good surveys of this period (in the New American Nation series) are Harold U. Faulkner, *Politics, reform and expansion, 1890–1900* (New York: Harper, 1959) **(B291)**, George E. Mowry, *The era of Theodore Roosevelt, 1900–1912* (New York: Harper, 1958) **(B292)**, and Arthur S. Link, *Woodrow Wilson and the Progressive Era, 1910–1917* (New York: Harper, 1954) **(B293)**.

Other studies of the reform movement that should be consulted are Robert H. Wiebe, *Businessmen and reform; a study of the progressive movement* (Cambridge, Mass.: Harvard Univ. Pr., 1962) **(B294)**, Gabriel Kolko, *The triumph of conservatism; a reinterpretation of American history, 1900–1916* (New York: Free Pr., 1963) **(B295)**, Richard Hofstadter, *The age of reform* (New York: Knopf, 1955) **(B296)**, Henry F. May, *The end of American innocence* (New York: Knopf, 1959) **(B297)**, and Eric F. Goldman, *Rendezvous with destiny* (New York: Knopf, 1952) **(B298)**.

FIGURE 36
Sources of Information in the Social Sciences

find the best reference books in any field of history in which you may be interested, you will want one kind of guide, like this one or Wood Gray. If, on the other hand, you want a comprehensive approach to the literature of a particular area, you will want a guide like Beers'.

Summary

1. There are two kinds of published guides to history.
2. The first discusses the discipline and how to carry out research in it.
3. The second is simply a list of the best books.

The human species, according to the best theory I can form of it, is composed of two distinct races, the men who borrow, and the men who lend.

Lamb, *Essays of Elia: The Two Races of Men.*

You have used bibliographies, the card catalog, essay and periodical indexes, and government documents. It is a satisfying search. The search can prove not-so-satisfying, however, if key items are not held in your library, and even the largest library cannot have all the material everyone wants. How do you cope with an important gap in your bibliography?

One way to deal with the situation is to exploit the resources you have at your disposal – to use, in other words, what your library *does* have, making the most of that. That is, indeed, a challenge worth meeting. But sometimes it becomes really necessary to reach beyond the confines of one library.

Borrowing Through Your Own Institution

Ask your reference librarian to explain to you the interlibrary loan procedures in your library. It is often possible to borrow books from other libraries and have articles photocopied from periodicals that your library does not have. This is one place where you really get the payoff for the care with which you have kept the records of your bibliographic search. Interlibrary loan procedures usually involve a careful substantiation, or verification, of the citation you submit for the book or article you want. If you have recorded on your 3 x 5 cards precisely in which bibliography or index you found the citation, you are far ahead of the game. One other hint on this type of loan: start it in motion well in advance of your deadline. Borrowing takes time, and you will need plenty of time to digest the book or article when it does arrive, before writing about it.

Taking a Trip

Don't rule out the possibility of travelling yourself to a neighboring library to use or borrow the item you need. Find out from your library whether the neighboring institution lends to students from outside its walls, and how easy it is to return material. You should also ask your librarian whether or not you will need a pass or letter of introduction.

Before you take such a jaunt, you will want to know whether or not the neighboring library has the periodical or book you need. The librarian can help you use *Union List of Serials; American Newspapers, 1821--1936: A Union List; New Serial Titles* and local lists to determine what periodicals are in other libraries. Books are similarly listed in the *National Union Catalog* with symbols indicating which libraries hold them. But the *NUC* symbols are incomplete and a phone call to the library you wish to visit is more reliable.

Using the *Library of Congress Catalog -- Books: Subjects*

The *National Union Catalog* lists by author books that have been cataloged in libraries all over the country. The *Library of Congress Catalog -- Books: Subjects* lists by subject the books that have been cataloged since 1950 by the world's largest library, the Library of Congress in Washington, DC. FIGURE 37 shows a sample page from that catalog under the subject heading "Woman – Suffrage – U.S." The catalog is published in five-year cumulations with quarterly

WOMAN (Continued)

—SUFFRAGE—U. S.

Adams, Mildred, 1894–
  The right to be people. [1st ed.] Philadelphia, Lippincott, 1967 [*1966]
  248 p. 22 cm.
  JK1896.A3   324.3   66–23241

Coolidge, Olivia E
  Women's rights; the suffrage movement in America, 1848–1920, by Olivia Coolidge. [1st ed.] New York, Dutton [1966]
  189 p. Illus., ports. 24 cm.
  JK1896.C6   324.30973   66–7977

Kraditor, Aileen S
  The ideas of the woman suffrage movement, 1890–1920 [by] Aileen S. Kraditor. New York, Columbia University Press, 1965.
  xii, 313 p. 23 cm.
  JK1896.K7   324.30973   65–14410

Porter, Kirk Harold, 1891–
  A history of suffrage in the United States, by Kirk H. Porter. New York, Greenwood Press [1969, *1918]
  xi, 260 p. 23 cm.
  JK1846.P82 1969   324'.73   69–14039
                                        MARC

Severn, William.
  Free but not equal; how women won the right to vote, by Bill Severn. New York, J. Messner [1967]
  189 p. Illus., ports. 22 cm.
  JK1896.S4   324'.3'0973   67–2770

Stanton, Elizabeth (Cady) 1815–1902, ed.
  History of woman suffrage. Edited by Elizabeth Cady Stanton, Susan B. Anthony, and Matilda Joslyn Gage. New York, Arno Press, 1969.
  6 v. Illus., maps, ports. 24 cm.
  JK1896.S8 1969   324'.3'09   73–79182
                                        MARC

FIGURE 37
Library of Congress Catalog -- Books: Subjects

supplements and provides you with a comprehensive list of books you might want to try to borrow from other libraries.

Of course, check the card catalog of any library you might be visiting on the chance of finding some new material not in your library.

Summary

1. Sometimes it is necessary to tap the resources of other institutions and there are several ways of accomplishing this.

2. You can request loans or photocopies from the other institutions. Ask your librarian for help in doing this. Have an exact citation of the item you want and a precise description of where you found it mentioned. Leave enough leeway so that you will not be rushed for time when using the book. In other words: borrow early.

3. You can visit neighboring libraries to use their resources, taking with you any introductory letters you will need and an understanding of their lending procedures.

4. The *Library of Congress Catalog -- Books: Subjects* provides a good clue to the books you might expect to find in other libraries.

Sed summa sequar fastigia rerum. (I will trace the outlines of the chief events.) Vergil, *Aeneid.*

Perhaps by the time you have finished your research you believe with George Eliot, "The happiest women, like the happiest nations, have no history." One hopes you are not left with a paper that reflects Lord Chesterfield's aphorism, "History is only a confused heap of facts."

What this book would like to have proven to you is that the writing of a historical paper, or at least the collecting of the material upon which you wish to base your paper, is an ordered process, and one which you ought to approach with the same care that you apply to putting together the ideas of your paper. In searching out sources, you will be helped by the order that the library has imposed on the wealth of printed material in its care. The ordered reference sources can signal to you the outlines of a search strategy to use in culling the best from the mass of material. Appendix I ex-plains and diagrams various strategies that can be used.

Amos Bronson Alcott was quite right when he said that "The richest minds need not large libraries." Learn to use your library with intelligence and care, and you will have learned a skill that will stand you in good stead throughout your life.

"Historians ought to be precise, faithful, and unprejudiced; and neither interest nor fear, hatred nor affection, should make them swerve from the way of truth," says Cervantes in *Don Quixote.* That level of objectivity is hard to attain, particularly when marks are at stake. So I leave you with one wish which, if you don't read Latin, can be translated at the library: "Historia quoquo modo scripta delectat." May your professor believe it!

Search Strategies for Term Papers in History

Each student develops his or her own habits and style for researching a paper, whether or not he or she recognizes them as such. The trick is to develop efficient, fruitful and conscious habits, ones that can be adapted to various papers on various topics. A careful strategy ensures relevance and reasonable thoroughness. It allows you to transfer the search methods you learn to other papers and to disciplines in which you may have little or no expertise. It provides a clear place to begin, and a clear place to end, your search.

There are three methods of searching for material for a paper, three search strategies, that appear singularly appropriate to history students. The first might be called the straight-line method, the second, the document-centered method, and the third, the citation method.

1. The straight-line method is a good one to use when you know little or nothing about your topic and have little or no material collected. It is a very thorough method and will probably net you plenty of resource material. Use it, therefore, when you are beginning with little, and want to locate a wide range of opinion and information.

The method begins with a summary article from an encyclopedia to give an overview of the topic, brief information about important people and dates, and a basic bibliography. You then begin the search for books on the topic, using guides, general bibliographies, specific bibliographies and footnotes. Next, the library's card catalog should be searched to yield all the books you can squeeze out of it. Thirdly, you need journal articles and to find those you use the most appropriate periodical indexes available. Finally, the *Essay and General Literature Index* will give you essays or short readings to round out your paper.

The straight-line method then looks thus:

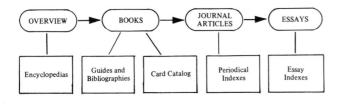

If this sounds familiar it may be because this is the method upon which this book is based.

2. The document-centered approach to a term paper cuts to the heart of the historical method, where that involves examining recorded history. This method begins with an historical document, with asking questions about it and its setting. For instance, we might choose the "Declaration of Sentiments" signed at the Seneca Falls Convention in 1848 and modeled after the "Declaration of Independence." What does it say? You can locate the text by using the documents collection, *Documents in American History*, edited by Henry Steele Commager (9th ed., New York: Appleton-Century-Crofts, 1973). What are some of the questions one can ask of such a document? One question is "Who penned it?" Another is "What personalities does it mention?" Both these questions are biographical questions and you would use all the *biographical sources* you have learned in order to answer it, e.g., *Dictionary of American Biography*. Another question to ask is "When was it said/written?" While a date is often given with the printed document, you can enlarge the scope of your answer to this question by consulting *chronologies* such as Neville Williams' *Chronology of the Modern World* (London: Barrie and Rockliff, 1966), which will tell you what other pertinent events were occurring at the same time or just prior to and after the writing of your document. A third question would be "For whom was this written?" and that may require a broad answer. *Encyclopedias and dictionaries* will often go a long way in answering it. A fourth question is "In what social, political, and/or artistic setting was this written?" Answers to that come through texts and articles for which you need to use *bibliographies and periodical indexes*. The final, perhaps largest, question is "What has become of the document since?" How has it been used? What has been made of it?" For the answers you will need to use almost the entire gamut of your searching expertise. *Encyclopedias, bibliographies, periodical indexes*, all will be useful to such a search.

You might diagram this search thus:

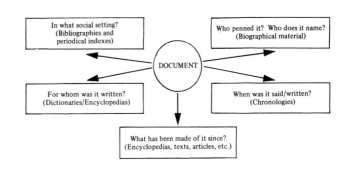

3. The final method of search appropriate to a term

paper is the citation method. Use this method when you have already come across the book or article that you would like to make the center of your search, when you have found one article or book highly relevant to your topic.

If what you have found is scholarly it will, no doubt, cite its sources of information and tell you on what research your prime author based his or her research. You should look up those sources and use them for more information or to place your author in perspective. You can check the cited authors' footnotes too, locating their sources of information. You have a basic bibliography already. But what about the scholars who have written since your prime author wrote? Have they cited your author? And if so, have they accepted, rejected, or commented upon the research? What has been written *since* on the topic? To trace this you use the *Social Sciences Citation Index* which you learned to use in Chapter 7, using FIGURE 24.

The citation method works backwards from a prime resource and then builds forward in time using a citation index. Diagrammed it might look thus:

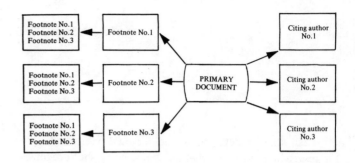

These three methods, (line, document-centered and citation) offer three search strategies. Use the one most appropriate to your needs, but try to get practice, at one time or another, in each of the three.

Regardless of which strategy you use, you should be keeping careful records of the material found and of where it was found as described in Chapter 1.

Appendix II

Library Knowledge Test

A. Directions: Use this catalog card to answer the questions below.

```
                    The Presidency of George Washington.


   E        McDonald, Forrest.
   311          The Presidency of George Washington.  Lawrence, Uni-
   M1.2      versity Press of Kansas [1974]
                xi, 210 p.  port.  23 cm.  (American Presidency series)

                Bibliography: p. 187-199.




             1. United States—Politics and government—1789-1797.  2. Wash-
          ington, George, Pres. U. S., 1732-1799.    I. Title.     Series.

          E311.M12                          973.4'1'0924  [B]        73-11344
          ISBN 0-7006-0110-4                                           MARC

          Library of Congress            73 [4]
```

1. Would this card be filed with other cards beginning "E," "M," "P," or "T"?
2. Does the book include a list of publications?
3. Under what other headings will cards for this book be found in the card catalog?

B. Directions: Use this excerpt from the *Readers' Guide to Periodical Literature* to answer the following questions.

4. How do you find the full title of the periodical that carries the article, "Legends in Stained Glass"?
5. On what page does it appear?
6. In what volume does it appear?
7. Who is the author of the article "Path as Clear as a Ray of Light"?
8. Does the article "George Washington's Trees" have any pictures?

WASHINGTON, George
George Washington's farewell address; September 17, 1796. Cong Digest 55:24-31 Ja '76

about
Button collecting. D. F. Brown. pors Hobbies 81:116-17 S '76 •
George Washington:
His role in the founding of a nation. Cong Digest 55:21-2+ Ja '76 •
Important dates in his career. Cong Digest 55:23+ Ja '76 •
George Washington dances. V. Huckenpahler. il por Dance Mag 50:44-7 Jl '76 •
George Washington slept here. . . E. Cheatham and P. Cheatham. il Travel 145:42-9 F '76 •
George Washington's trees. H. Clepper. il Am For 82:22-5 Ag '76 •
Heritage: Mount Vernon. il House & Gard 148: 40-7 Jl '76 •
Legends in stained glass. M. E. Marty. Chr Cent 93:447 My 5 '76 •
Man behind the myths. H. LaFav. il Nat Geog 150:90-111 Jl '76 •
Mirror for presidents. F. McDonald. Commentary 62:34-41 D '76 •
Mutiny in Washington's army. L. Gragg. il map Am Hist Illus 11:34-43 O '76 •
Our first real national folk hero! P. W. Schmidtchen. il pors Hobbies 80:134-6+ F; 81:134-5 Mr '76 •
Path as clear as a ray of light. il por Time Sp S 26, 1789 issue 107:11-12+ [My 17 '76] •
Washington the statesman. W. McKinley. il pors Sat Eve Post 248:42-3 Jl '76 •

The answers are at the bottom of the next page.

Answers to the Library Knowledge Test:

1. P. 2. Yes. (The bibliography is on pages 187–199).
3. a) McDonald, Forrest. b) United States -- Politics and
government–1789-1797. c) Washington, George, Pres. U.S.,
1732-1799. 4. The title is spelled out in the front of the
Readers' Guide. 5. Page 447. 6. Volume 93. 7. Anonymous. 8. Yes. ("il" is the abbreviation of "illustrated").

Since question three has three answers, a perfect score is
10. If you got only 7 or 8 correct, you probably need to
spend time with the library guides mentioned in the Preface.
If you got less than 7 correct answers, be sure to study those
guides before proceeding with this book.

Basic Reference Sources for

Courses in History

Note: The first library search with any of the following course-related bibliographies will be easier if used in conjunction with Appendix 4, "Guidelines for Proceeding." The basic work on this bibliography was completed in 1977. Then it was updated by adding new titles found in the *American Reference Books Annual* through the 1979 volume. However, time did not permit searching for post-1977 editions of older titles. A * indicates a title described in the text.

Outline of Classified Bibliography

I. Ancient History
   A. Encyclopedias and Dictionaries
   B. Bibliographies
   C. Atlases

II. Medieval History
   A. Encyclopedia
   B. Bibliographies
   C. Atlases
   D. Chronology

III. Modern History
   A. Encyclopedias and Dictionaries
   B. Bibliographies
   C. Atlas
   D. Chronologies

IV. North American History
   A. Encyclopedias and Dictionaries
   B. Bibliographies
      1. General
      2. By Period
      3. Labor History
      4. Economic and Business History
      5. History of Education
      6. Religious History
      7. Military History
      8. Diplomatic History
      9. Constitutional History
      10. Demography
      11. Women's History
      12. Immigrant and Ethnic History
      13. American Indian History
      14. Black History
      15. Mexican-American History
      16. Puerto Rican History
      17. Autobiographies, Diaries, Travel Accounts
      18. Historical Fiction
   C. Periodical Indexes
   D. Newspaper Index
   E. Book Review Sources
   F. Biographical Sources
   G. Atlases
      1. Historical
      2. General
   H. Chronologies
   I. Statistics
   J. Government Documents
   K. Documents Collections
   L. Periodicals

V. History of the British Isles
   A. Dictionaries
   B. Bibliographies
      1. By Period
      2. Local History
      3. General
   C. Periodical Index
   D. Newspaper Indexes
   E. Biographical Sources
   F. Atlases
   G. Chronology
   H. Historical Statistics
   I. Government Documents
   J. Documents Collections

VI. European History
   A. Encyclopedias and Dictionaries
   B. Bibliographies
   C. Book Review Source
   D. Biographical Sources
   E. Atlases
   F. Historical Statistics
   G. Government Documents
   H. Documents Collections

VII. Russian, East European and Balkan States History
   A. Encyclopedias, Handbooks, and Dictionaries

I. Ancient History

  A. Encyclopedias and Dictionaries
    Avery, Catherine B. *The New Century Classical Handbook*. New York: Appleton-Century-Crofts, 1962. 1162 pp.
    The Cambridge Ancient History. Cambridge: Cambridge University Press, 1970-- (Multi-volume with extensive bibliographies.)
    Oxford Classical Dictionary. N.G.L. Hammond

and H.H. Scullard, eds. 2d ed. Oxford: Clarendon Press, 1970. 1198 pp.

The Princeton Encyclopedia of Classical Sites. Richard Stillwell and others, eds. Princeton, NJ: Princeton University Press, 1976. 1041 pp.

Woodcock, Percival George. *Concise Dictionary of Ancient History.* New York: Philosophical Library, 1955. 465 pp.

B. Bibliographies

Bengtson, Herman. *Introduction to Ancient History.* Translated from the 6th ed. Berkeley: University of California Press, 1970. 221 pp.

Chambers, Mortimer. *Greek and Roman History.* 2d ed. Washington, DC: Service Center for Teachers, 1965. 47 pp. (Service Center for Teachers, Publication no. 11.)

Classical World Bibliography of Greek and Roman History, by Walter Donlan. New York: Garland, 1977. 234 pp.

Goodwater, Leanna. *Women in Antiquity: An Annotated Bibliography.* Metuchen, NJ: Scarecrow, 1975. 171 pp.

International Guide to Classical Studies. Darien, CT: American Bibliographic Service, 1961– .

C. Atlases

Beek, Martinus A. *Atlas of Mesopotamia: A Survey of the History and Civilisation of Mesopotamia from the Stone Age to the Fall of Babylon.* London: Nelson, 1962. 164 pp.

Everyman's Classical Atlas. 3d ed. London: Dent; New York: Dutton, 1961. 195 pp.

Heyden, A.A.M. van der, and H.H. Scullard. *Atlas of the Classical World.* New York: Thomas Nelson, 1959. 221 pp.

McEvedy, Colin. *The Penguin Atlas of Ancient History.* Harmondsworth: Penguin Books, 1967. 96 pp.

II. Medieval History

A. Encyclopedia

Cambridge Medieval History. Cambridge: Cambridge University Press, 1911–1936. 8 vols. (Has extensive bibliographies.)

B. Bibliographies

Atiya, Aziz Suryal. *The Crusade: Historiog-*

raphy and Bibliography. Bloomington: Indiana University Press, 1962. 170 pp.

Davis, Ralph H.C. *Medieval European History, 395--1500: A Select Bibliography.* 2d rev. ed. London: Historical Association, 1968. 48 pp.

International Guide to Medieval Studies. v. 1– . Darien, CT: American Bibliographic Service, 1961– .

International Medieval Bibliography. 1967– . Leeds, Eng.: University of Leeds, 1967– . Semiannual. Originally in card form.

Paetow, Louis J. *A Guide to the Study of Medieval History.* Rev. ed. Millwood, NY: Kraus Reprint Corp., 1959. (Reprint of 1931 edition.) 670 pp. (With supplement update by Gray C. Boyce, Medieval Academy of America, 1962.)

Powell, James M., ed. *Medieval Studies: An Introduction.* Syracuse, NY: Syracuse University Press, 1976. 389 pp.

Thompson, James W. *Reference Studies in Medieval History.* 3d ed. Chicago: University of Chicago Press, 1923–1924. 3 vols.

C. Atlases

East, William G. *An Historical Geography of Europe.* 5th ed. London: Methuen, 1966. 492 pp.

Meer, Frederik van der. *Atlas of Western Civilization.* 2d ed. Princeton, NJ: Van Nostrand, 1960. 240 pp.

D. Chronology

Storey, R.L. *Chronology of the Medieval World, 800--1491.* New York: David McKay, 1973. 717 pp.

III. Modern History

A. Encyclopedias and Dictionary

Morris, Richard B. and Graham W. Irwin. *Harper Encyclopedia of the Modern World: A Concise Reference History from 1760 to the Present.* New York: Harper & Row, 1970. 1303 pp.

New Cambridge Modern History. Cambridge: University Press, 1957–1970. 14 vols. (14th volume is atlas volume.) Unlike the older *Cambridge Modern History* (13 vols., 1902–1926), still valuable for its bibliographies, the newer volumes contain no extensive bibliographies. You may use the intended supplement to the series for this purpose: John Roach, ed. *A Bibliography of Modern History*. London: Cambridge University Press, 1968. 412 pp.

Palmer, Alan W. *A Dictionary of Modern History, 1789--1945*. London: The Cresset Press, 1962. 314 pp.

B. Bibliographies

Blackey, Robert, *Modern Revolutions and Revolutionists*. Santa Barbara, CA: ABC–Clio, 1976. 285 pp.

Bloomberg, Marty and Hans Weber. *World War II and Its Origins: A Select Annotated Bibliography of Books in English*. Littleton, CO: Libraries Unlimited, 1975. 328 pp.

Krikler, Bernard and Walter Laqueur, eds. *A Reader's Guide to Contemporary History*. Chicago: Quadrangle Books, 1972. 259 pp.

C. Atlas

McEvedy, Colin. *The Penguin Atlas of Modern History (to 1815)*. Harmondsworth: Penguin Books, 1972. 97 pp.

D. Chronologies

Williams, Neville. *Chronology of the Expanding World: 1492 to 1762*. New York: David McKay, 1969. 700 pp.

Williams, Neville. *Chronology of the Modern World: 1763 to the Present Time*. Rev. ed. New York: David McKay, 1968. 923 pp.

IV. North American History

A. Encyclopedias and Dictionaries

* Adams, James Truslow. *Dictionary of American History*. Rev. ed. New York: Chas. Scribner's Sons, 1976--8. 8 vols.

Encyclopedia Canadiana. Toronto: Grolier of Canada, 1975. 10 vols.

Johnson, Thomas H., ed. *Oxford Companion to American History*. New York: Oxford University Press, 1966. 906 pp.

Morris, Richard B. and Jeffrey B. Morris, eds. *Encyclopedia of American History*. Bicentennial edition. New York: Harper & Row, 1976. 1259 pp.

Sperber, Hans and Travis Trittschuh. *American Political Terms: An Historical Dictionary*. Detroit: Wayne State University Press, 1962. 516 pp.

Story, Norah. *The Oxford Companion to

Canadian History and Literature. New York: Oxford University Press, 1967. 946 pp. Supplement, 1973.

Webster's Guide to American History. Charles Van Doren and Robt. McHenry, eds. Springfield, MA: G. & C. Merriam, 1971. 1428 pp.

Wentworth, Harold and Stuart B. Flexner. *Dictionary of American Slang*. 2d ed. New York: Thomas Y. Crowell, 1975. 774 pp.

B. Bibliographies

1. General

Beers, Henry Putney. *Bibliographies in American History; Guide to Materials for Research*. Rev. ed. New York: Wilson, 1942. 502 pp.

Cassara, Ernest. *History of the United States of America: A Guide to Information Sources*. Detroit: Gale Research, 1977. 459 pp.

* *Harvard Guide to American History*. Rev. ed. Frank Freidel, ed. Cambridge, MA: Belknap Press, 1974. 2 vols. (This work has had a distinguished history. An earlier edition was edited by Oscar Handlin, Arthur Meier Schlesinger, Samuel Eliot Morison, Frederick Merk, Arthur Meier Schlesinger, Jr. and Paul H. Buck. Even earlier, as *Guide to the Study and Reading of American History* and as *Guide to the Study of American History*, the editors included Albert Bushnell Hart, Edward Channing and Frederick Jackson Turner.)

Howes, Wright. *U.S.--iana 1650--1950: A Selective Bibliography*. Rev. ed. New York: Bowker for the Newberry Library, 1962. 652 pp.

Sharp, Harold S. *Footnotes to American History; A Bibliographic Source Book*. Metuchen, NJ: Scarecrow, 1977. 639 pp.

* U.S. Library of Congress. General Reference and Bibliography Division. *A Guide to the Study of the United States of America: Representative Books Reflecting the Development of American Life and Thought*. Donald H. Mugridge, Blanche P. McCrum and Roy Prentice Basler, eds. Washington, DC: U.S. Government Printing Office, 1960. 1193 pp. Also *Supplement, 1956--1965*. 1976. 526 pp.

2. By Period

Bremner, Robert H. *American Social History Since 1860*. New York: Appleton-Century-Crofts, 1971. 140 pp.

* DeSantis, Vincent P. *The Gilded Age, 1877--1896*. Northbrook, IL: AHM Publishing Co., 1973. 168 pp.

Donald, David. *The Nation in Crisis, 1861--1877*. New York: Appleton-Century-Crofts, 1969. 107 pp.

Fehrenbacher, Don E. *Manifest Destiny and the Coming of the Civil War, 1841--1861*. New York: Appleton-Century-Crofts, 1970. 143 pp.

Ferguson, E. James. *Confederation, Constitution, and Early National Period, 1781--1815*. Northbrook, IL: AHM Publishing Corp., 1975. 191 pp.

Greene, Jack P. *The American Colonies in the Eighteenth Century, 1689--1763*. New York: Appleton-Century-Crofts, 1969. 152 pp.

Grob, Gerald N. *American Social History Before 1860*. New York: Appleton-Century-Crofts, 1970. 153 pp.

Link, Arthur S. and William M. Leary, Jr. *The Progressive Era and the Great War, 1896--1920*. New York: Appleton-Century-Crofts, 1969. 95 pp.

Nevins, Allan. *Civil War Books: A Critical Bibliography*. Baton Rouge: Louisiana State University Press, 1967–1968. 2 vols.

Shy, John. *The American Revolution*. Northbrook, IL: AHM Publishing Corp., 1973. 151 pp.

Smith, Dwight L. and Terry A. Simmerman, eds. *Era of the American Revolution: A Bibliography*. Santa Barbara, CA: ABC–Clio, 1975. 395 pp.

U.S. Library of Congress. General Reference and Bibliography Division. *The American Revolution: A Selected Reading List*. Washington, DC, 1968. 42 pp.

Vaughan, Alden T. *The American Colonies in the Seventeenth Century*. New York: Appleton-Century-Crofts, 1971. 165 pp.

Winther, Oscar O. *A Classified Bibliography of the Periodical Literature of the Trans-Mississippi West (1811--1957)*. Bloomington: Indiana University Press, 1961. 626 pp.

Also consult the many bibliographies dealing with the local history of particular states.

3. Labor History

McBrearty, James C. *American Labor History and Comparative Labor Movements: A Selected Bibliography*. Tucson: AZ: University of Arizona Press, 1973. 271 pp.

Neufeld, Maurice F. *A Representative Bibliography of American Labor History*. Ithaca, NY: New York State School of Industrial and Labor Relations, Cornell University, 1964. 146 pp.

Rose, Fred D. *American Labor in Journals of History: A Bibliography*. Champaign: University of Illinois, Institute of Labor and Industrial Relations, 1962. 91 pp.

Stroud, Gene S. and Gilbert E. Donahue, eds. *Labor History in the United States: A General Bibliography*. Urbana: University of Illinois, Institute of Labor and Industrial Relations, 1961. 167 pp.

4. Economic and Business History

Kirkland, Edward C. *American Economic History Since 1860*. New York: Appleton-Century-Crofts, 1971. 91 pp.

Larson, Henrietta M. *Guide to Business History*. Cambridge, MA: Harvard University Press, 1948. 1207 pp.

Lovett, Robert W. *American Economic and Business History Information Sources: An Annotated Bibliography of Recent Works Pertaining to Economic, Business, Agricultural and Labor History and the History of Science and Technology for the United States and Canada*. Detroit: Gale Research, 1971. 323 pp.

Orsagh, Thomas et al. *The Economic History of the United States Prior to 1860: An Annotated Bibliography*. Santa Barbara, CA: ABC–Clio, 1975. 113 pp.

Taylor, George R. *American Economic History Before 1860*. New York: Appleton-Century-Crofts, 1969. 122 pp.

5. History of Education

Herbst, Jurgen. *The History of American Education*. Northbrook, IL: AHM Publishing Corp., 1973. 168 pp.

6. Religious History

Burr, Nelson R. *A Critical Bibliography of Religion in America*. Princeton, NJ: Princeton University Press, 1961. 2 vols.

Burr, Nelson R. *Religion in American Life*. New York: Appleton-Century-Crofts, 1971. 190 pp.

7. Military History

Albion, Robert G. *Maritime & Naval History: An Annotated Bibliography*. 4th ed. Newton Abbot, Eng.: David & Charles, 1973. 379 pp.

8. Diplomatic History

Bemis, Samuel F. and Grace G. Griffin. *Guide to the Diplomatic History of the United States, 1775--1921*. Washington, DC: U.S. Government Printing Office, 1935. 996 pp.

The Foreign Affairs 50-Year Bibliography: New Evaluations of Significant Books on International Relations 1920--1970. New York: Published for the Council on Foreign Relations by R.R. Bowker, 1972. 964 pp.

Fowler, Wilton B. *American Diplomatic History Since 1890*. Northbrook, IL: AHM Publishing Corp., 1975. 190 pp.

Trask, David F. et al., eds. *A Bibliography of United States -- Latin American Relations Since 1810*. Lincoln: University of Nebraska Press, 1968. 474 pp.

9. Constitutional History

Mason, Alpheus T. and D. Grier Stephenson, Jr. *American Constitutional Development*. Arlington Heights, IL: AHM, 1977. 184 pp.

Millett, Stephen M. *A Selected Bibliography of American Constitutional History*. Santa Barbara, CA: ABC-Clio, 1975. 128 pp.

10. Demography

Dubester, Henry J. *State Censuses: An Annotated Bibliography of Censuses of Population Taken after the Year 1790 by States and Territories of the United States*. Washington, DC: U.S. Government Printing Office, 1948. 78 pp.

11. Women's History

The Common Women Collective. *Women in U.S. History: An Annotated Bibliography*. Cambridge, MA, 1976. 114 pp.

* Jacobs, Sue-Ellen. *Women in Perspective: A Guide for Cross-Cultural Studies*. Urbana, IL: University of Illinois Press, 1974. 315 pp.

* Krichmar, Albert. *The Women's Rights Movement in the United States, 1848--1970: A Bibliography and Sourcebook*. Metuchen, NJ: Scarecrow Press, 1972. 445 pp.

* Rosenberg, Marie B. and Len V. Bergstrom. *Women and Society: A Critical Review of the Literature with a Selected Annotated Bibliography*. Beverly Hills: Sage, 1975--1978. 2 vols.

Soltow, Martha Jane and Mary K. Wery. *American Women and the Labor Movement, 1825--1974: An Annotated Bibliography*. Metuchen, NJ: Scarecrow Press, 1976. 247 pp.

White, Cynthia L., ed. *Women's Magazines, 1693--1968*. London: Michael Joseph, 1970. 350 pp.

12. Immigrant and Ethnic History

Miller, Wayne Charles. *A Comprehensive Bibliography for the Study of American Minorities*. New York: New York University Press, 1976. 2 vols.

13. American Indian History

Josephy, Alvin M., Jr. *The Indian Heritage of America*. New York: Knopf, 1968. 397 pp.

Prucha, Francis Paul. *A Bibliographical Guide to the History of Indian-White Relations in the United States*. Chicago: University of Chicago Press, 1977. 454 pp.

Smith, Dwight L. *Indians of the United States and Canada: A Bibliography*. Santa Barbara, CA: ABC-Clio, 1974. 470 pp.

14. Black History

Dumond, Dwight L. *A Bibliography of Antislavery in America*. Ann Arbor: University of Michigan Press, 1961. 119 pp.

McPherson, James M. et al. *Blacks in America: Bibliographical Essays*. Garden City, NY: Doubleday, 1971. 452 pp.

Miller, Elizabeth W. and Mary L. Fisher, comp. *The Negro in America: A Bibliography*. 2d ed. Cambridge, MA: Harvard University Press, 1970. 371 pp.

Salk, Erwin A. *A Layman's Guide to Negro History*. New ed. New York: McGraw-Hill, 1967. 214 pp.

Smith, Dwight L. *Afro-American History: A Bibliography*. Santa Barbara, CA: ABC-Clio, 1974. 872 pp.

Work, Monroe Nathan. *A Bibliography of the Negro in Africa and America*. New York: Wilson, 1928. 698 pp.

15. Mexican-American History

Nogales, Luis G., ed. *The Mexican-American: A Selected and Annotated Bibliography*. 2d ed. Stanford: Stanford University Press, 1971. 174 pp.

Pino, Frank. *Mexican Americans: A Research Bibliography*. East Lansing: Latin American Studies Center, Center for International Programs, Michigan State University, 1974. 2 vols.

Trejo, Arnulfo. *Bibliographia Chicana: A Guide to Information Sources*. Detroit: Gale Research, 1975. 213 pp.

Woods, Richard D. *Reference Materials on Mexican Americans: An Annotated Bibliography*. Metuchen, NJ: Scarecrow, 1976. 197 pp.

16. Puerto Rican History

Bravo, Enrique R., comp. *An Annotated, Selected Puerto Rican Bibliography*. New York: Urban Center of Columbia University, 1972. 118 pp.

Cordasco, Francesco, ed. *Puerto Ricans on the United States Mainland*. Totowa, NJ: Rowman and Littlefield, 1972. 160 pp.

Vivo, Paquita. *The Puerto Ricans: An Annotated Bibliography*. New York: Bowker, 1973. 312 pp.

17. Autobiographies, Diaries, Travel Accounts

Clark, Thomas D., ed. *Travels in the Old South: A Bibliography*. Norman: University of Oklahoma Press, 1948--1959. 4 vols. (Also his *Travels in the New South*, 1962. 2 vols.)

Coulter, E. Merton. *Travels in the Confederate States, a Bibliography*. Norman: University of Oklahoma Press, 1948. 289 pp.

Hubach, Robert R. *Early Midwestern Travel Narratives: An Annotated Bibliography, 1634--1850*. Detroit: Wayne State University Press, 1961. 159 pp.

Kaplan, Louis et al. *A Bibliography of American Autobiographies*. Madison: University of Wisconsin Press, 1961. 384 pp.

Matthews, William and Roy Harvey Pearce. *American Diaries: An Annotated Bibliography of American Diaries Written Prior to the Year 1861*. Berkeley and Los Angeles: University of California Press, 1945. 397 pp.

18. Historical Fiction

Baker, Ernest A. *A Guide to Historical Fiction*. New York: Macmillan, 1914. 580 pp.

Irwin, Leonard B. *Guide to Historical Fiction for the Use of Schools, Libraries, and the General Reader*. 10th ed. Brooklawn, NJ: McKinley, 1971. 262 pp.

Van Derhoof, Jack. *A Bibliography of Novels Related to American Frontier and Colonial History*. Troy, NY: Whitston, 1971. 509 pp.

C. Periodical Indexes

* *America: History and Life*. v. 0-- , 1954-- . Santa Barbara, CA: ABC--Clio, 1964-- .

* *Writings on American History*. 1902--1903, 1906--1940, 1948--1960, 1962/73, 1973/74-- . Washington, DC; Millwood, NY: The American Historical Association and Kraus--Thompson Organization, 1904--1972, 1974-- .

D. Newspaper Index

* *New York Times Index*. 1851-- . New York: New York Times, 1913-- . (Earlier volumes have been reprinted by R.R. Bowker, New

York.)

E.   Book Review Sources

*   *America: History and Life; Part B: Index to Book Reviews*, v. 11-- . Santa Barbara, CA: ABC--Clio, 1974-- . Seven times per year.
*   *Reviews in American History*. v. 1-- . Westport, CT: Redgrave Information Resources 1973-- . Quarterly.
*   *Writings on American History, 1906--39/40*. Publisher varies, 1908--44. No reviews indexed after 1940.

F.   Biographical Sources

     Biographical Directory of the American Congress, 1774--1971. Washington, DC: U.S. Government Printing Office, 1971. 1972 pp.
*   *Dictionary of American Biography*. New York: Scribner's, 1928--1958. 10 vols. (Also supplements.)
     Dictionary of Canadian Biography. Toronto: University of Toronto Press, 1966-- .
*   *Directory of American Scholars*. 7th ed. New York: Edited by Jaques Cattell Press, R.R. Bowker, 1978. 4 vols.
*   *National Cyclopaedia of American Biography*. Clifton, NJ: James T. White, 1893-- . 47 vols. with current volumes A-- , 1930-- .
*   *Notable American Women, 1607--1950: A Biographical Dictionary*. Edward T. James, ed. Cambridge, MA: Belknap Press of Harvard University Press, 1971. 3 vols.
*   *Who Was Who in America*. 1897/1942-- . Chicago: Marquis Who's Who, 1943-- . (Also *Who Was Who in America: Historical Volume, 1607--1896*. Chicago, 1963.)
*   *Who's Who in America: A Biographical Dictionary of Notable Living Men and Women*. 1899-- . Chicago: Marquis Who's Who, 1899-- . Biennial.
     Who's Who of American Women: A Biographical Dictionary. 1958/59-- . Chicago: Marquis Who's Who, 1958-- . Biennial.

G.   Atlases

     1.   Historical

          Adams, James T. and R.V. Coleman, eds. *Atlas of American History*. New York: Scribner's, 1943. 360 pp.
          Atlas of the American Revolution. Edited by Kenneth Nebenzahl and Don Higginbotham. New York: Rand McNally, 1974. 218 pp.
          Cappon, Lester J., ed. *Atlas of Early American History: The Revolutionary Era 1760--1790*. Princeton, NJ: Princeton University Press, 1976. 157 pp.
          Esposito, Vincent J., ed. *The West Point Atlas of American Wars*. New York: Praeger, 1959. 2 vols.
          Gaustad, Edwin S. *Historical Atlas of Religion in America*. New York: Harper & Row, 1962. 179 pp.
          Kerr, Donald G.G. and C.C.J. Bond. *A Historical Atlas of Canada*. 3d rev. ed. Toronto: Thomas Nelson, 1975. 100 pp.
          Lord, Clifford L. and Elizabeth H. Lord. *Historical Atlas of the United States*. Rev. ed. New York: Henry Holt, 1953. 238 pp.
          Paullin, Charles O. *Atlas of the Historical Geography of the United States*. Washington, DC: Published jointly by Carnegie Institute of Washington and the American Geographical Society, 1932. 162 pp.

     2.   General

          The National Atlas of Canada. 4th ed. Toronto: Macmillan Co. of Canada in association with the Dept. of Energy, Mines and Resources, and Information, 1974. 254 pp.
          The National Atlas of the United States of America. Washington, DC: United States Dept. of the Interior, Geological Survey, 1970. 430 pp.
          Oxford Regional Economic Atlas: United States and Canada. Oxford: Oxford University Press, 1975. 175 pp.

H.   Chronologies

     Carruth, Gorton. *The Encyclopedia of American Facts and Dates*. 5th ed. New York: Crowell, 1970. 854 pp.

I.   Statistics

     Dodd, Donald B. and Wynell S. Dodd. *Historical Statistics of the United States, 1790--1970*. University, AL: University of Alabama Press, 1973-- . 4 vols.
     Taeuber, Irene B. and Conrad Taeuber. *People of the United States in the 20th Century*. Washington, DC: U.S. Government Printing

Office, 1972. 1083 pp.

U.S. Bureau of the Budget. *Statistical Services of the United States Government.* Rev. ed. Washington, DC: U.S. Government Printing Office, 1968. 156 pp. (Useful for discovering which agency of the government collects what current statistics.)

U.S. Bureau of the Census. *Historical Statistics of the United States, Colonial Times to 1970.* Bicentennial Edition. Washington, DC: U.S. Government Printing Office, 1975. 2 vols.

U.S. Bureau of the Census. *The Statistical Abstract of the United States.* 1878-- . Washington, DC: U.S. Government Printing Office, 1879-- . Annual.

U.S. National Vital Statistics Division. *Vital Statistics of the United States.* 1937-- . Washington, DC: U.S. Government Printing Office, 1939-- . Annual. (Supersedes *Mortality Statistics* and *Birth, Stillbirth and Infant Mortality Statistics.*)

Urquhart, M.C. and Kenneth A.H. Buckley. *Historical Statistics of Canada.* New York: Cambridge University Press; Toronto: Macmillan, 1965. 672 pp.

J.   Government Documents

CIS/Annual: Congressional Information Service. 1970-- . Washington, DC: The Service, 1971-- . Monthly.

CQ Weekly Report. 1945-- . Washington, DC: Congressional Quarterly, 1945-- . Weekly. (Cumulates into *Congressional Quarterly Almanac,* 1945-- .)

*   *Catalogue of the Public Documents of the United States, 1893--1940.* Washington, DC: U.S. Government Printing Office, 1896--1945. 25 vols.

Checklist of United States Public Documents, 1789--1909. 3d ed. Washington, DC: U.S. Government Printing Office, 1911. 1707 pp.

Congress and the Nation. v. 1-- . Washington, DC: Congressional Quarterly, 1965-- . (v. 1, 1945-1964; v. 2, 1965-1968; v. 3, 1969--1972; v. 4, 1973--1976.)

*   *Congressional Record: United States Congress.* 1873-- . Washington, DC: U.S. Government Printing Office, 1973-- . Daily when Congress is in session.

Jackson, Ellen P., comp. *Subject Guide to Major United States Government Publications.* Chicago: American Library Association, 1968. 185 pp.

Lu, Joseph K. *U.S. Government Publications Relating to the Social Sciences: A Selected Annotated Guide.* Beverly Hills, CA: Sage, 1975. 260 pp. (Includes a detailed chapter for American History.)

*   *Monthly Catalog of United States Government Publications.* 1895-- . Washington, DC: U.S. Government Printing Office, 1895-- . Monthly. (Preceded by *Catalogue of the Public Documents . . .* See above.)

*   Morehead, Joe. *Introduction to United States Public Documents.* 2d ed. Littleton, CO: Libraries Unlimited, 1978. 377 pp.

Numerical Lists and Schedule of Volumes of the Reports and Documents of the 73rd-- Congress. 1933/34-- . Washington, DC: U.S. Government Printing Office, 1934-- .

*   Schmeckebier, Laurence F. and Roy B. Eastin. *Government Publications and Their Use.* 2d rev. ed. Washington, DC: The Brookings Institution, 1969. 510 pp.

Wynkoop, Sally. *Subject Guide to Government Reference Books.* Littleton, CO: Libraries Unlimited, 1972. 276 pp.

K.   Documents Collections

Commager, Henry Steele. *Documents of American History.* 9th ed. New York: Appleton-Century-Crofts, 1973. 2 vols. in 1.

Historic Documents. 1972-- . Washington, DC: Congressional Quarterly, 1973-- . (Includes some foreign and international documents.)

Treaties and Other International Acts of the United States of America. Washington, DC: U.S. Government Printing Office, 1931-- .

Treaties and Other International Agreements of the United States of America, 1776--1949. Washington, DC: U.S. Government Printing Office, 1968--1976. 13 vols.

U.S. President. *Compilation of the Messages and Papers of the Presidents.* James D. Richardson, ed. Washington, DC: Bureau of National Literature and Art, 1917. 20 vols. Updated vols. also published.

U.S. President. *Public Papers of the Presidents of the United States.* Washington, DC: U.S. Government Printing Office, 1958-- .

L.   Periodicals

Crouch, Milton and Hans Raum, comps. *Directory of State and Local History Periodicals.* Chicago: American Library Association, 1977. 124 pp.

V.   History of the British Isles

A.   Dictionaries

Low, Sir Sidney J.M., ed. *The Dictionary of English History*. New ed. London: Cassell, 1928. 1154 pp.

Steinberg, Sigfrid H. et al., eds. *Steinberg's Dictionary of British History*. 2d ed. New York: St. Martin's, 1971. 421 pp.

B.   Bibliographies

1.   By Period

Abbott, Wilbur C. *A Bibliography of Oliver Cromwell*. Cambridge, MA: Harvard University Press, 1929. 551 pp.

Altholz, Josef L. *Victorian England 1837--1901*. Cambridge: University Press, 1970. 100 pp.

Altschul, Michael. *Anglo-Norman England, 1066--1154*. London: Cambridge University Press, 1969. 83 pp.

Bonser, Wilfrid. *An Anglo-Saxon and Celtic Bibliography, 450--1087*. Berkeley: University of California Press, 1957. 2 vols.

Brown, Lucy M. and Ian R. Christie, eds. *Bibliography of British History, 1789--1851*. Oxford, Eng.: Clarendon Press, 1977. 790 pp.

Clemoes, Peter. *Anglo-Saxon England*. v. 1-- . New York: Cambridge University Press, 1972-- .
(Each annual includes a bibliography of Anglo-Saxon studies published during the year.)

Elton, G.R. *Modern Historians on British History, 1485--1945: A Critical Bibliography, 1945--1969*. Ithaca, NY: Cornell University Press, 1970. 239 pp.

Gipson, Lawrence H. *A Bibliographical Guide to the History of the British Empire, 1748--1776*. New York: Knopf, 1968. 478 pp.

Graves, Edgar B. *A Bibliography of English History to 1485: Based on the Sources and Literature of English History from the Earliest Times to about 1485 by Charles Gross*. Oxford: Clarendon Press, 1975. 1103 pp.

Guth, DeLoyd J. *Late-Medieval England, 1377--1485*. Cambridge: Cambridge University Press, 1976. 154 pp.

Hanham, H.J., ed. *Bibliography of British History, 1851--1914*. Oxford: Clarendon Press, 1976. 1634 pp.

Havighurst, Alfred F. *Modern England, 1901--1970*. Cambridge: Cambridge University Press, 1976. 119 pp.

Higham, Robin. *A Guide to the Sources of British Military History*. Hamden, CT: Archon Books, 1975. 559 pp.

Keeler, Mary F., ed. *Bibliography of British History: Stuart Period, 1603--1714*. 2d ed. New York: Oxford University Press, 1970. 734 pp.

Levine, Mortimer. *Tudor England 1485--1603*. Cambridge: University Press, 1968. 115 pp.

Morgan, William T. and Chloe S. Morgan. *Bibliography of British History (1700--1715) with Special Reference to the Reign of Queen Anne*. Bloomington, IN: Indiana University Press, 1934--1942. 5 vols.

New York. Public Library. *A List of Works Relating to Scotland*. George F. Black, comp. New York, 1916. 1233 pp.

Pargellis, Stanley and D.J. Medley, eds. *Bibliography of British History: The Eighteenth Century, 1714--1789*. Oxford: Clarendon Press, 1951. 642 pp.

Read, Conyers, ed. *Bibliography of British History: Tudor Period, 1485--1603*. 2d ed. Oxford: Clarendon Press, 1959. 624 pp.

Sachse, William L. *Restoration England, 1660--1689*. New York: Cambridge University Press, 1971. 114 pp.

Wales. University. Board of Celtic Studies. History and Law Committee. *A Bibliography of the History of Wales*. 2d ed. Cardiff: University of Wales Press, 1962. 330 pp.

Williams, Judith B. *A Guide to the Printed Materials for English Social and Economic History, 1750--1850*. New York: Columbia University Press, 1926. 2 vols.

2.   Local History

Stephens, W.B. *Sources for English Local History*. Manchester, Eng.: Manchester University Press, 1973. 260 pp.

3.   General

Annual Bibliography of British and Irish History. 1975-- . Atlantic Highlands, NJ: Humanities Press for the Royal

Historical Society, 1976-- . Annual.

British Museum. Dept. of Printed Books. *General Catalogue of Printed Books.* v. 1- . London: Trustees, 1931- . Earlier vols., as *Catalogue of Printed Books . . .* , were published between the years 1881–1900 (95 vols.) and 1900–1905 (13 vols.).

Chaloner, W.H. and R.C. Richardson. *British Economic and Social History: A Bibliographical Guide.* Totowa, NJ: Rowman and Littlefield, 1976. 129 pp.

Moody, Theodore Wm., ed. *A New History of Ireland.* Oxford: Clarendon Press, 1976-- . 9 vols. (Vol. 9 is a general bibliography.)

Munro, Donald J. *Writings on British History, 1946--48.* London: University of London, Institut. of Hist. Research, 1973. 635 pp.

Rose, John H., Arthur P. Newton and Ernest A. Benians. *Cambridge History of the British Empire.* Cambridge: Cambridge University Press, 1929--1959. 8 vols.
(Bibliographies published at the end of each volume.)

Royal Historical Society. *Writings on British History, 1901--33.* v. 1-- . London: J. Cape, 1968-- .

Sims, John M. *Writings on British History, 1952--54.* London: University of London, Institute of Historical Research, 1975. 365 pp.

C. Periodical Index

British Humanities Index. 1962-- . London: The Library Association, 1962-- .
(Formerly *Subject Index to Periodicals,* 1915/16--1961.)

D. Newspaper Indexes

Palmer's Index to the Times Newspaper, 1790--June 1941. London: Palmer, 1868--1943.

Times, London. *Index to the Times.* 1906-- . London: Times, 1907-- .
(Research Publications, Woodbridge, CT, have recently announced the republication of the indexes to the *Times* newspaper for the years 1785-- .)

E. Biographical Sources

Crone, John S. *Concise Dictionary of Irish Biography.* Rev. and enl. ed. Dublin: Talbot; New York: Longmans, 1937. 290 pp.

* *Dictionary of National Biography.* Rev. ed. London: Smith, Elder; New York: Macmillan, 1908--1909. Leslie Stephen and Sidney Lee, eds. 22 vols. (Also Supplements, Oxford Univ. Press, 1920-- .)

Dictionary of Welsh Biography Down to 1940 . . . . Oxford: Blackwell, 1959. 1157 pp.

Donaldson, Gordon and Robert S. Morpeth. *Who's Who in Scottish History.* New York: Barnes & Noble, 1974. 254 pp.

Riddell, Edwin, ed. *Lives of the Stuart Age, 1603--1714.* Newly rev. ed. Laurence Urdang Assoc., comps. New York: Barnes & Noble, 1976. 511 pp.
(Others in series are *Lives of the Tudor Age, 1485--1603, Lives of the Georgian Age, 1714--1837* and, in preparation, *Lives before the Tudors* and *Lives of the Victorian Age.*)

Stenton, Michael. *Who's Who of British Members of Parliament: A Biographical Dictionary of the House of Commons Based on Annual Volumes of Dod's Parliamentary Companion and Other Sources.* 1832/1885-- . Atlantic Highlands, NJ: Humanities, 1976-- .

* *Who Was Who.* 1897/1915-- . London: Adam and Chas. Black, 1929-- .

* *Who's Who.* 1849-- . New York: St. Martin's Press, 1949-- .

Who's Who, What's What and Where in Ireland. New York: Macmillan Information, 1973. 736 pp.

F. Atlases

Edwards, Ruth D. *An Atlas of Irish History.* London: Methuen, 1974. 261 pp.

Gilbert, Martin. *British History Atlas.* London: Weidenfeld and Nicolson, 1968. 118 pp.

An Historical Geography of England Before A.D. 1800. Cambridge: Cambridge University Press, 1936. 566 pp.

G. Chronology

Powicke, Frederick M. and E.B. Fryde. *Handbook of British Chronology.* 2d ed. London: Royal Historical Society, 1961. 565 pp.

H. Historical Statistics

Great Britain. Central Statistical Office. *Annual*

Abstract of Statistics. v. 1-- , 1840/53-- . London: Statistical Office, 1854-- . Annual.

Mitchell, B.R. and Phyllis Deane. *Abstract of British Historical Statistics.* Cambridge: Cambridge University Press, 1962. 588 pp. (Also *Second Abstract of British Historical Statistics.* 1971. 227 pp.)

Whitaker, Joseph. *An Almanack.* v. 1-- . London: Whitaker, 1869-- . Annual.

I.   Government Documents

Bond, Maurice F. *Guide to the Records of Parliament.* London: H.M.S.O., 1971. 352 pp.

Ford, Percy and G. Ford. *A Breviate of Parliamentary Papers, 1900--1916: The Foundation of the Welfare State.* Oxford: Basil Blackwell, 1957. 470 pp. (Rev. reprint: Shannon, Ire.: Irish University Press, 1969.)

Ford, Percy and G. Ford. *A Breviate of Parliamentary Papers, 1917--1939.* Oxford: Basil Blackwell, 1951. 571 pp. (Rev. reprint: Shannon, Ire.: Irish University Press, 1969.)

Ford, Percy and G. Ford. *A Breviate of Parliamentary Papers, 1940--1954: War and Reconstruction.* Oxford: Basil Blackwell, 1961. 515 pp.

Ford, Percy and G. Ford. *A Guide to Parliamentary Papers: What They Are and How to Find Them, How to Use Them.* 3d ed. Shannon, Ire.: Irish University Press, 1972. 87 pp.

Ford, Percy and G. Ford. *Select List of British Parliamentary Papers, 1833--1899.* Oxford: Basil Blackwell, 1953. 165 pp. (Rev. reprint: Shannon, Ire.: Irish University Press, 1969.)

Ford, Percy and Diana Marshallsay. *Select List of British Parliamentary Papers, 1955--1964.* Shannon, Ire.: Irish University Press, 1970. 117 pp. (Volume for 1965--74 in preparation, KTO Press.)

Hansard's Catalogue and Breviate of Parliamentary Papers, 1696--1834. Oxford: Blackwell, 1953. 234 pp.

J.   Documents Collections

Baxter, Stephen B. *Basic Documents of English History.* Boston: Houghton Mifflin, 1968. 338 pp.

Curtis, Edmund and Robert B. McDowell. *Irish Historical Documents, 1172--1922.*
London: Methuen, 1943. 331 pp.

English Historical Documents. v. 1-- . New York: Oxford University Press, 1953-- .

Stephenson, Carl and Frederick G. Marcham, eds. *Sources of English Constitutional History.* Rev. ed. New York: Harper & Row, 1972. 2 vols. (Vol. 1, 600 A.D. -- Interregnum; Vol. 2, Interregnum -- Present.)

VI.   European History

A.   Encyclopedias and Dictionaries

Brockhaus Enzyklopädie in zwanzig Bänden. Siebzehnte völlig neubearbeitete Auflage des Grossen Brockhaus. Wiesbaden: Brockhaus, 1966--1974. 20 vols.

Cooke, James J. *France 1789--1962.* Newton Abbot: David & Charles; Hamden, CT: Archon Books, 1975. 287 pp.

Enciclopedia Italiana di Scienze, Lettere ed Arti. Roma: Istit. della Enciclopedia Italiana, 1928--1937. 36 vols. (Also Appendice I, 1938; Appendice II, 1949; Appendice III, 1961.)

Enciclopedia Universal Ilustrada Euopeo-Americana. Barcelona, Espasa, 1907--33. 80 vols. in 81. Supplements, 1934-- .

Gardner, Edmund G. *Italy: A Companion to Italian Studies.* London: Methuen, 1934. 274 pp.

Grand Larousse Encyclopédique en Dix Volumes. Paris: Librairie Larousse, 1960--1964. 10 vols. (Also Supplements, 1968, 1975.)

Roeder, William S. *Dictionary of European History.* New York: Philosophical Library, 1954. 324 pp.

B.   Bibliographies

Bromley, John S. and A. Goodwin. *A Select List of Works on Europe and Europe Overseas, 1715--1815.* Oxford: Clarendon Press, 1956. 144 pp.

Conover, Helen F. *Introduction to Europe: A Selective Guide to Background Reading.* Washington, DC: Library of Congress, 1950. 201 pp. (Supplement, 1955.)

Davies, Alun. *Modern European History, 1494--1788: A Select Bibliography.* London: Historical Association, 1967. 39 pp.

Deutsch Bibliographie. Wöchetliches Verzeichnis. Frankfurt a.M.: Buchhändler-Vereinigung GMBH, 1947-- .

Deutsche Nationalbibliographie. Leipzig: Börsenverein der Deutschen Buchhändler, 1931-- .

Deutsches Bücherverzeichnis. v. 1-- . Leipzig: VEB Verlag für Buchund Bibliothekswesen, 1915-- .

Dorn, Georgette M. *Latin America, Spain and Portugal: An Annotated Bibliography of Paperback Books.* 2d rev. ed. Washington, DC: Library of Congress, 1976. 328 pp.

Howard, Donald D. *The French Revolution and Napoleon Collection at Florida State University: A Bibliographical Guide.* Tallahassee, FL: Friends of the Florida State Library, Strozier Library, Florida State University, 1973. 426 pp.

Paris. Bibliothèque Nationale. *Catalogue Générale des Livres Imprimes: Auteurs.* v. 1--220. Paris: Imprimerie Nationale, 1970--1974. 220 vols. (In progress. Supplements cover other years.)

Pasley, J. M. S. *Germany: A Companion to German Studies.* New ed. London: Methuen, 1972. 678 pp.

Ragatz, Lowell J. *A Bibliography for the Study of European History, 1815 to 1939.* Ann Arbor, MI: Edwards Bros., 1942. 286 pp. (Also: Supplements.)

Robinson, Jacob. *The Holocaust and After; Sources & Literature in English.* Jerusalem: Israel Universities Press, 1973. 353 pp.

Stachura, Peter D. *The Weimar Era and Hitler, 1918--1933; A Critical Bibliography.* Oxford, Eng.: Clio, 1977. 275 pp.

C. Book Review Source

Reviews in European History: A Journal of Criticism -- the Renaissance to the Present. v. 1-- . Westport, CT: Redgrave Information Resources Corp., 1974-- . Quarterly.

D. Biographical Sources

Allgemeine Deutsche Biographie. Leipzig: Duncker, 1875--1912. 56 vols.

Dictionnaire de Biographie Française. v. 1-- . Paris: Letouzey, 1933-- .

Neue Deutsche Biographie. v. 1-- . Berlin: Duncker and Humblot, 1953-- .

Who's Who in Germany. 1956-- . Munich, Oldenbourg, 1955-- . Irregular.

E. Atlases

Boussard, Jacques. *Atlas Historique et Culturel de la France.* Paris: Elsevier, 1957. 214 pp.

Fox, Edward W. and H.S. Deighton. *Atlas of European History.* New York: Oxford University Press, 1957. 64 pp.

Oxford Regional Economic Atlas: Western Europe. London: Oxford University Press, 1971. 96 pp.

F. Historical Statistics

Mitchell, B.R. *European Historical Statistics 1750--1970.* New York: Columbia University Press, 1975. 847 pp.

Statistical Pocket Book of the Germany Democratic Republic. v. 1-- , 1959-- . Berlin: Staatsverlag, 1959-- . Annual.

Statistics for individual countries can be located in statistical annuals often published in official compendiums, such as *Annuaire Statistique de la France,* 1878-- . Annual.

G. Government Documents

Childs, James B. *German Federal Republic Official Publications, 1949--1957 . . . .* Washington, DC: Library of Congress, Reference Dept., Serial Div., 1958. 887 pp.

Dampierre, Jacques de. *Les Publications Officielles des Pouvoirs Publics: Étude Critique at Administrative.* Paris: Picard, 1942. 628 pp.

H. Documents Collections

Kertesz, G.A. *Documents in the Political History of the European Continent 1815--1939.* Oxford: Clarendon Press, 1968. 507 pp.

VII. Russian, East European and Balkan States History

A. Encyclopedias, Handbooks, and Dictionaries

Great Soviet Encyclopedia. v. 1-- . 3d ed. A.M. Prokhorov, ed. New York: Macmillan, 1973-- . (A translation of *Bolshaia Sovetskaia entsiklopediia,* 3d ed.)

McGraw-Hill Encyclopedia of Russia and the Soviet Union. Michael T. Florinsky, ed. New York: McGraw-Hill, 1961. 624 pp.

Pushkarev, Sergei G. *Dictionary of Russian Historical Terms from the Eleventh Century to 1917.* New Haven: Yale University Press, 1970. 199 pp.

Slavonic Encyclopaedia. Joseph S. Roucek, ed. New York: Philosophical Library, 1949. 1445 pp.

Soviet Union and Eastern Europe: A Hand-

book. George Schöpflin, ed. New York: Praeger, 1970. 714 pp.

B. Bibliographies

ABSEES: Soviet and East European Abstract Series. v. 1-- , July 1970-- . Glasgow, Scot.: University of Glasgow, Institute of Soviet and East European Studies, 1970-- .

American Bibliography of Slavic and East European Studies. 1967-- . Columbus: Ohio State University Press, 1972-- . (Supersedes *American Bibliography of Russian and East European Studies, 1956--1966.*)

Byrnes, Robert F. *Bibliography of American Publications on East Central Europe, 1945--1957.* Bloomington, IN: Indiana University Press, 1958. 213 pp.

Carr, Edward H. *A History of Soviet Russia.* v. 1-- . London: Macmillan, 1950-- . (This is not a bibliography, but contains good bibliographies.)

Columbia University. Russian Institute. *Russian and Soviet Studies: A Handbook.* Preliminary edition. Columbus, OH: American Association for the Advancement of Slavic Studies, 1973. 219 pp.

Crowther, Peter A. *A Bibliography of Works in English on Early Russian History to 1800.* Oxford: Blackwell, 1969. 236 pp.

Grierson, Philip. *Books on Soviet Russia, 1917--1942: A Bibliography and Guide to Reading.* London: Methuen, 1943. 358 pp.

Horak, Stephen M. *Junior Slavica: A Selected Annotated Bibliography of Books in English on Russia and Eastern Europe.* Rochester, NY: Libraries Unlimited, 1968. 244 pp.

Horecky, Paul L. *Basic Russian Publications: An Annotated Bibliography on Russia and the Soviet Union.* Chicago: University of Chicago Press, 1962. 313 pp.

Horecky, Paul L. *East Central Europe: A Guide to Basic Publications.* Chicago: University of Chicago Press, 1969. 956 pp.

Horecky, Paul L. *Russia and the Soviet Union: A Bibliographic Guide to Western Language Publications.* Chicago: University of Chicago Press, 1965. 473 pp.

Horecky, Paul L. *Southeastern Europe: A Guide to Basic Publications.* Chicago: University of Chicago Press, 1969. 755 pp.

Pierce, Richard A. *Soviet Central Asia: A Bibliography.* Berkeley: Center for Slavic and East European Studies, University of California, 1966. 3 pts.

Russian Studies, 1941--1958: A Cumulation of the Annual Bibliographies from the Russian Review. Thomas Schultheiss, ed. Ann Arbor, MI: Pierian, 1972. 395 pp.

Shapiro, David. *A Select Bibliography of Works in English on Russian History, 1801--1917.* Oxford: Blackwell, 1962. 106 pp.

Stavrianos, Leften S. *The Balkans Since 1453.* New York: Holt, Rinehart and Winston, 1958. 991 pp. (Includes extensive bibliography.)

Strakhovsky, Leonid I. *A Handbook of Slavic Studies.* Cambridge, MA: Harvard University Press, 1949. 774 pp.

C. Newspaper Index

Current Digest of the Soviet Press. v. 1– , Feb. 1, 1949– . New York: Joint Committee on Slavic Studies, 1949– .

D. Biographical Sources

Institut zur Erforschung der UdSSR. *Who Was Who in the USSR.* Metuchen, NJ: Scarecrow Press, 1972. 677 pp.

Prominent Personalities in the USSR. Metuchen, NJ: Scarecrow Press for the Institute for the Study of the USSR, 1968. 792 pp. Quarterly supplements.

Who's Who in the USSR. 1961/62–1965/66. Montreal: Intercontinental, 1962--1966. 2 vols.

E. Atlases

1. Historical

Adams, Arthur E. et al. *An Atlas of Russian and East European History.* New York: Praeger, 1967. 204 pp.

Gilbert, Martin. *Russian History Atlas.* New York: Macmillan, 1972.

Historical Atlas of the USSR. New York: C.S. Hammond, 1950. 3 vols.

2. General

Goodall, George. *Soviet Union in Maps.* London: George Philip, 1954. 32 pp.

Oxford Regional Economic Atlas: USSR and Eastern Europe. London: Oxford University Press, 1969. 142 pp.

F. Statistics

Mickiewicz, Ellen P. *Handbook of Soviet Social*

Science Data. New York: Free Press, 1973. 225 pp.

Russia. Tsentral'noe Statisticheskoe Upravlenie. *Statistical Handbook of the USSR: with . . . additional tables and annotations . . . .* Moscow, 1956; New York: National Industrial Conference Board, 1957. 122 pp. (Translation of *Narodnoe Khoziaistvo SSSR.*)

VIII. Near and Middle Eastern, and North African History

A. Encyclopedias

Concise Encyclopaedia of Arabic Civilization: The Arab East. Stephan and Nandy Ronart, eds. New York: Praeger, 1960. 589 pp.

Concise Encyclopaedia of Arabic Civilization: The Arab West. Stephan and Nandy Ronart, eds. New York: Praeger, 1966. 410 pp.

Encyclopaedia Judaica. Jerusalem: Encyclopaedia Judaica; New York: Macmillan, 1972. 16 vols.

Encyclopaedia of Islam. New ed. B. Lewis and J. Schacht, eds. Atlantic Highlands, NJ: Humanities Press, 1960– . (5 vols. when complete.)

Encyclopedia of Zionism and Israel. Raphael Patai, ed. New York: Herzl Press, 1971. 2 vols.

The International Jewish Encyclopedia. Ben Isaacson and Deborah Wigoder, eds. Englewood Cliffs, NJ: Prentice-Hall, 1973. 336 pp.

B. Bibliographies

Alexander, Yonah. *Israel: Selected, Annotated and Illustrated Bibliography.* Gilbertsville, NY: Victor Buday, 1968. 116 pp.

Atiyeh, George N. *The Contemporary Middle East 1948–1973: A Selective and Annotated Bibliography.* Boston: G.K. Hall, 1975. 690 pp.

Birnbaum, Eleazar. *Books on Asia from the Near East to the Far East: A Guide for the General Reader.* Toronto: University of Toronto, 1971. 356 pp.

The Cambridge History of Islam. P.M. Holt, Ann K.S. Lambton and Bernard Lewis, eds. Cambridge: University Press, 1970. 2 vols.

Davidson, Roderic H. *The Near and Middle East: An Introduction to History and Bibliography.* Washington, DC: Service Center for Teachers of History, 1959. 48 pp.

DeVore, Ronald M. *The Arab-Israeli Conflict; A Historical, Political, Social & Military Bibliography.* Santa Barbara, CA: Clio, 1976. 273 pp.

Howard, Harry N. *The Middle East: A Selected Bibliography of Recent Works, 1960–1970.* Rev. by Jay Fuller. Washington, DC: Middle East Institute, 1972. 68 pp. Supplements, 1970–1972 (1972), 1972–1973 (1973), 1973–1974 (1974).

Howard, Harry N. et al. *Middle East and North Africa: A Bibliography for Undergraduate Libraries.* Williamsport, PA: Bro-Dart, 1971. 98 pp.

el-Khalidi, Walid and Jill Khadduri, eds. *Palestine and the Arab-Israeli Conflict; An Annotated Bibliography.* Beirut: Institute for Palestine Studies, 1974. 736 pp.

Littlefield, David W. *The Islamic Near East and North Africa: An Annotated Guide to Books in English for Non-Specialists.* Littleton, CO: Libraries Unlimited, 1977. 376 pp.

Macro, Eric. *Bibliography of the Arabian Peninsula.* Coral Gables, FL: University of Miami Press, 1958. 80 pp.

Zuwiyya, Jalal. *The Near East (South-west Asia and North Africa): A Bibliographic Study.* Metuchen, NJ: Scarecrow, 1973. 392 pp.

C. Biographical Sources

Who's Who in the Arab World. Ed. 1– . Beirut: Editions Publitec, 1965– . Irregular.

D. Atlases

Beek, Martinus A. *Atlas of Mesopotamia: A Survey of the History and Civilization of Mesopotamia from the Stone Age to the Fall of Babylon.* London: Nelson, 1962. 164 pp.

Gilbert, Martin. *Jewish History Atlas.* 2d ed. London: Weidenfeld and Nicolson, 1976. 135 pp.

Hazard, Harry W., ed. *Atlas of Islamic History.* 3d ed. Princeton, NJ: Princeton University Press, 1954. 49 pp.

Roolvink, Roelof, et al. *Historical Atlas of the Muslim Peoples.* Cambridge, MA: Harvard University Press, 1957. 40 pp.

Vilnay, Zer. *The New Israel Atlas: Bible to Present Day.* Jerusalem: Israel Universities Press, 1968; New York: McGraw-Hill, 1969. 112 pp.

E. Chronology

Freeman-Grenville, Greville S.P. *The Muslim and Christian Calendars, Being Tables for the Conversion of Muslim and Christian Dates from the Hijra to the Year A.D. 2000.* 2d ed. London: Rex Collings, 1977. 95 pp.

F. Documents Collection

al-Marayati, Abid A. *Middle Eastern Constitutions and Electoral Laws.* New York: Praeger, 1968. 483 pp.

IX. History of Africa South of the Sahara

A. Encyclopedias, Handbooks, and Dictionaries

Africa South of the Sahara. Sahara. Ed. 1-- . London: Europa Publications, 1971-- . Annual.

The Cambridge History of Africa. v. 1-- . Cambridge, Eng.: Cambridge University Press, 1970-- .

Hartwig, Gerald W. and William M. O'Barr. *The Student Africanist's Handbook: A Guide to Resources.* Cambridge, MA: Schenkman, 1974. 160 pp.

The New Africans: A Guide to the Contemporary History of Emergent Africa and Its Leaders, Written by Fifty Correspondents of Reuters New Agency. Sidney Taylor, ed. New York: Putnam, 1967. 504 pp.

Rosenthal, Eric. *Encyclopaedia of Southern Africa.* 5th ed. London and New York: Frederick Warne, 1970. 653 pp.

Standard Encyclopaedia of Southern Africa. v. 1–12. Cape Town: Nasionale Opvoedkundige Uitgewery Bpk., 1970–1975(?).

Wilson, Monica H. and Leonard Thompson. *The Oxford History of South Africa.* New York: Oxford University Press, 1969–1971. 2 vols. (Bibliographies at end of each volume.)

The "African Historical Dictionary" series published by Scarecrow Press includes historical dictionaries on individual countries in Africa, e.g., Dhomey (1975), Somalia (1975).

B. Bibliographies

Bridgeman, Jon and David E. Clarke. *German Africa, A Select Annotated Bibliography.* Stanford, CA: Hoover Institution on War, Revolution and Peace, 1965. 120 pp.

Conover, Helen F. *Africa South of the Sahara: A Selected, Annotated List of Writings.* Washington, DC: Library of Congress, 1963. 354 pp.

A Current Bibliography on African Affairs. v. 1– . Farmingdale, NY: Baywood Publishing Co., 1962– . (Published for the African Bibliographic Center.)

Duignan, Peter. *Africa South of the Sahara: A Bibliography for Undergraduate Libraries.* Williamsport, PA: Bro-Dart, 1971. 128 pp.

Duignan, Peter and L.H. Gann. *A Bibliographical Guide to Colonialism in Sub-Saharan Africa.* Cambridge: Cambridge University Press, 1973. 552 pp. (Volume 5 of *Colonialism in Africa, 1870--1960.*)

Duignan, Peter and Helen F. Conover. *Guide to Research and Reference Works on Sub-Saharan Africa.* Stanford, CA: Hoover Institution Press, 1971. 1102 pp.

Glazier, Kenneth M. *Africa South of the Sahara: A Select and Annotated Bibliography, 1958--1963.* Stanford, CA: Hoover Institution on War, Revolution and Peace, 1964. 65 pp.

Glazier, Kenneth M. *Africa South of the Sahara: A Select and Annotated Bibliography, 1964--1968.* Stanford, CA: Hoover Institution Press, 1969. 139 pp.

Gutkind, Peter and John B. Webster. *A Select Bibliography on Traditional and Modern Africa.* Syracuse, NY: Syracuse University Press, 1968. 323 pp.

Hogg, Peter C. *The African Slave Trade and Its Suppression: A Classified and Annotated Bibliography of Books, Pamphlets and Periodical Articles.* London: Cass, 1973. 409 pp.

Muller, C.F.J., F.A. Van Jaarsveld, and Theo Van Wijk. *A Select Bibliography of South African History: A Guide for Historical Research.* Pretoria: University of South Africa, 1966. 215 pp.

Paden, John N. and Edward W. Soja. *The African Experience.* Evanston, IL: Northwestern University Press, 1970. 4 vols. (Volume 3a is a bibliography, and volume 3b is a guide to resources.)

Thompson, Leonard M., Richard Elphick and Inez Jarrick. *Southern African History Before 1900: A Select Bibliography of Articles.* Stanford, CA: Hoover Institution Press, 1971. 102 pp.

U.S. Library of Congress. European Affairs Div. *Introduction to Africa: A Selective Guide to Background Reading.* Helen F. Conover, comp. Washington, DC: University Press of Washington, DC, 1952. 237 pp.

C. Atlases

Clark, John D. *Atlas of African Prehistory*. Chicago: University of Chicago Press, 1967. 62 pp.

Fage, J.D. *An Atlas of African History*. Reprinted with amendments. London: E. Arnold, 1965. 64 pp.

Freeman-Grenville, Greville S.P. *A Modern Atlas of African History*. London: Rex Collings, 1976. 63 pp.

X. Asian History

A. Encyclopedia and Handbook

Wilber, Donald N. *The Nations of Asia*. New York: Hart, 1966. 605 pp.

Wint, Guy. *Asia: A Handbook*. New York: Praeger, 1966. 856 pp.

B. Bibliographies

American Oriental Society. Library. *Catalog of the Library*. Elizabeth Stout, ed. New Haven, CT: Yale University Press, 1930. 308 pp.

Bibliography of Asian Studies. 1966– . Chicago: Association for Asian Studies, 1967– . Annual. (Issued as 5th number of each volume of the *Journal of Asian Studies*. From 1936–1955 the bibliography appeared in *Far Eastern Quarterly*.)

Birnbaum, Eleazar. *Books on Asia from the Near East to the Far East: A Guide for the General Reader*. Toronto: University of Toronto Press, 1971. 356 pp.

Embree, Ainslee T. et al. *Asia: A Guide to Paperbacks*. Rev. ed. New York: The Asia Society, 1968. 181 pp.

Gillian, Donald G. et al. *East Asia: A Bibliography for Undergraduate Libraries*. Williamsport, PA: Bro-Dart, 1970. 130 pp.

Nunn, G. Raymond. *Asia: A Selected and Annotated Guide to Reference Works*. Cambridge, MA: The M.I.T. Press, 1971. 236 pp.

Quan, Lau-King. *Introduction to Asia: A Selective Guide to Background Reading*. Washington, DC: Library of Congress, 1955. 224 pp.

C. Atlas

Sellman, Roger R. *An Outline Atlas of Eastern History*. London: E. Arnold, 1954. 63 pp.

D. Chronology

Akiyama, Aisaburo. *A Chronological List of Japan and China*. 2d ed. New York: Paragon Book Reprint Co., 1964. 42 pp.

E. Documents Collection

Constitutions of Asian Countries. Bombay: N.M. Tripathi Private, 1968. 1179 pp.

XI. South Asian History

A. Encyclopedias and Dictionary

Balfour, Edward G. *Cyclopaedia of India and of Eastern and Southern Asia . . . .* 3d ed. London: Quaritch, 1885. 3 vols.

Bhattacharya, Sachchidananda. *A Dictionary of Indian History*. New York: Braziller, 1967. 888 pp.

Cambridge History of India. Cambridge: University Press, 1922–1937. 5 vols., numbered 1, 3, 4, 5, 6. (Includes bibliographies.)

B. Bibliographies

Abernethy, George L. *Pakistan: A Selected, Annotated Bibliography*. 4th ed. Davidson, NC: Publications Office, Davidson College, 1974. 53 pp.

Case, Margaret H. *South Asian History, 1750-- 1950: A Guide to Periodicals, Dissertations and Newspapers*. Princeton, NJ: Princeton University Press, 1968. 561 pp.

Chicago. University. College. *South Asia: An Introductory Bibliography: Introduction to the Civilization of India*. Maureen L.P. Patterson and Ronald B. Inden, eds. Chicago: University of Chicago Press, 1962. 412 pp.

Crane, Robert D. *The History of India: Its Study and Interpretation*. 2d ed. Washington, DC: Service Center for Teachers of History, 1965. 46 pp.

Jacob, Louis A. et al. *South Asia: A Bibliography for Undergraduate Libraries*. Williamsport, PA: Bro-Dart, 1970. 119 pp.

Mahar, J. Michael. *India: A Critical Bibliography*. Tucson: University of Arizona Press, 1964. 119 pp.

U.S. Dept. of the Army. *South Asia and the Strategic Indian Ocean: A Bibliographic*

Survey of Literature. Washington, DC: Dept. of the Army, 1973. 388 pp.

C. Biographical Source

Buckland, C.E. *Dictionary of Indian Biography*. London: Swan Sonnenschein, 1906. 494 pp.

D. Atlas

Davies, Cuthbert C. *An Historical Atlas of the Indian Peninsula*. 2d ed. Madras: Oxford University Press, 1959. 94 pp.

E. Chronologies

Burgess, James. *The Chronology of Modern India for Four Hundred Years from the Close of the Fifteenth Century. A.D. 1494--1894*. Edinburgh: Grant, 1913. 483 pp.

Rickmars, C. Mabel Duff. *The Chronology of India, from the Earliest Times to the Beginning of the Sixteenth Century*. Westminster: Constable, 1889. 409 pp.

Sharma, Jagdish Saran. *India Since the Advent of the British, a Descriptive Chronology from 1600 to Oct. 2, 1969*. Delhi: S. Chand, 1970. 817 pp.

F. Documents Collection

Mukhopadhyaya (or Mukherji), Panchananadasa. *Indian Constitutional Documents (1600--1918)*. 2d ed. Calcutta: Thacker, Spink, 1918. 2 vols.

XII. Southeast Asian History

A. Bibliographies

Bixler, Paul. *Southeast Asia: Bibliographic Directions in a Complex Area*. Middletown, CT: Choice, 1974. 106 pp.

Chen, John H.M. *Vietnam: A Comprehensive Bibliography*. Metuchen, NJ: Scarecrow Press, 1973. 314 pp.

Hay, Stephen and Margaret Case. *Southeast Asian History: A Bibliographic Guide*. New York: Praeger, 1962. 138 pp.

Hobbs, Cecil C. *Southeast Asia: An Annotated Bibliography of Selected Reference Sources in Western Languages*. Rev. ed. Washington, DC: Orientalia Division, Reference Dept., Library of Congress, 1964. 180 pp.

Johnson, Donald Clay et al. *Southeast Asia:*

A Bibliography for Undergraduate Libraries. Williamsport, PA: Bro-Dart, 1970. 77 pp.

Leitenberg, Milton and Richard D. Burns. *The Vietnam Conflict: Its Geographical Dimensions, Political Traumas, and Military Developments*. Santa Barbara, CA: ABC-Clio, 1973. 189 pp. (Includes a large section on history.)

Morrison, Gayle and Stephen Hay. *A Guide to Books on Southeast Asian History, 1961--1966*. Santa Barbara, CA: ABC-Clio, 1969. 105 pp. (Supplements Hay and Case above, except that "articles and dissertations are not included here.")

Tregonning, Kennedy G. *Southeast Asia: A Critical Bibliography*. Tucson: University of Arizona Press, 1969. 103 pp.

U.S. Dept. of the Army. *Peninsular Southeast Asia: A Bibliographic Survey of Literature: Burma, Cambodia, Laos, Thailand*. Washington, DC: Dept. of the Army, 1972. 435 pp.

U.S. Library of Congress. Reference Dept. *Indochina: A Bibliography of the Land and People*. Washington, DC, 1950. 367 pp.

XIII. Chinese History

A. Encyclopedia, Handbook, and Yearbook

China Yearbook, 1937/43-- . Taipei, Taiwan: China Publishing Co., 1943-- . Irregular.

The Encyclopaedia Sinica. Samuel Couling, ed. Shainghai: Kelly and Walsh; London; New York: Oxford University Press, 1917. 633 pp.

Wu, Yuan-li. *China: A Handbook*. New York: Praeger, 1973. 915 pp.

B. Bibliographies

Hucker, Charles O. *China: A Critical Bibliography*. Tucson: University of Arizona Press, 1962. 135 pp.

Hucker, Charles O. *Chinese History: A Bibliographic Review*. Washington, DC: Service Center for Teachers of History, 1958. 42 pp.

McCutcheon, J.M. *China and America: A Bibliography of Interactions, Foreign and Domestic*. Honolulu: University of Hawaii Press, 1972. 75 pp.

Posner, Arlene and Arne J. de Keijzer. *China: A Resource and Curriculum Guide*. Chicago: University of Chicago Press, 1973. 292 pp. (Includes a section listing and annotating major books on the history of China.)

U.S. Dept. of the Army. *Communist China: A Bibliographic Survey*. Washington, DC: Dept. of the Army, 1971. 263 pp.

Weitzman, David L. *Chinese Studies in Paperback*. Berkeley, CA: McCutchan, 1967. 88 pp.

C. Biographical Sources

Boorman, Howard L. *Biographical Dictionary of Republican China*. New York: Columbia University Press, 1967--1971. 4 vols.

Giles, Herbert A. *A Chinese Biographical Dictionary*. London: Wuaritch; Shanghai: Kelly and Walsh, 1898. 1022 pp.

Klein, Donald W. and Anne B. Clark. *Biographical Dictionary of Chinese Communism, 1921–1965*. Cambridge, MA: Harvard University Press, 1971. 2 vols.

Perleberg, Max. *Who's Who in Modern China (from the Beginning of the Chinese Republic to the end of 1953)*. Hong Kong: Ye Olde Printerie, 1954. 428 pp.

U.S. Dept. of State. Bureau of Intelligence and Research. *Directory of Chinese Communist Officials, 1953--1969*. Washington, DC: U.S. Government Printing Office, 1953--1969. 3 vols.

U.S. Dept. of State. Bureau of Intelligence and Research. *Directory of Officials of the People's Republic of China*. 1972-- . Washington, DC, 1972-- .

U.S. Library of Congress. Orientalia Division. *Eminent Chinese of the Ch'ing Period (1644--1912)*. Arthur W. Hummel, ed. Washington, DC: U.S. Government Printing Office, 1943--1944. 2 vols.

Who's Who in Communist China. Ed. 1-- . Hong Kong: Union Research Institute, 1966-- .

D. Atlases

Herrimann, Albert, ed. *An Historical Atlas of China*. New ed. Chicago: Aldine, 1966. 120 pp.

U.S. Central Intelligence Agency. *People's Republic of China Atlas*. Washington, DC: U.S. Government Printing Office, 1971. 82 pp.

E. Chronologies

Cheng, Peter. *A Chronology of the People's Republic of China from October 1, 1949*. Totawa, NJ: Littlefield, Adams, 1972.

364 pp.

Moule, Arthur C. *The Rulers of China, 221 B.C. -- A.D. 1949: Chronological Tables*. New York: Praeger, 1957. 154 pp.

XIV.   Japanese and Korean History

A. Dictionaries

Goedertier, Joseph M. *A Dictionary of Japanese History*. New York: Walker/Weatherill, 1968. 415 pp.

Papinot, Edmond. *Historical and Geographical Dictionary of Japan*. New York: Ungar, 1964. 2 vols.

B. Bibliographies

Gompertz, G. St. G.M. *Bibliography of Western Literature on Korea from Earliest Times until 1950*. Seoul: Don--A Publishing, 1963. 263 pp.

Hall, John W. *Japanese History: New Dimensions of Approach and Understanding*. Washington, DC: American Historical Association, 1961. 63 pp.

Henthorn, William E. *A Guide to Reference and Research Materials on Korean History: An Annotated Bibliography*. Honolulu: East-West Center, 1968. 152 pp.

Jones, Helen D. and Robin L. Winkler. *Korea: An Annotated Bibliography of Publications in Western Languages*. Washington, DC: Reference Dept., Library of Congress, 1950. 155 pp.

Silberman, Bernard S. *Japan and Korea: A Critical Bibliography*. Tucson: University of Arizona Press, 1962. 120 pp.

U.S. Dept. of the Army. *Communist North Korea: A Bibliographic Survey, 1971*. Washington, DC: U.S. Government Printing Office, 1971. 140 pp.

U.S. Dept. of the Army. *Japan: Analytical Bibliography with Supplementary Research Aids*. Washington, DC, 1972. 381 pp.

U.S. Library of Congress. Reference Dept. *Korea: An Annotated Bibliography*. Washington, DC, 1950. 3 vols. (Volume 1: Publications in Western Languages.)

Ward, Robert E. and Frank J. Shulman. *The Allied Occupation of Japan, 1945--1952: An Annotated Bibliography of Western-Language Materials*. Chicago, IL: American Library Association, 1974. 887 pp.

C. Newspaper Index

Elrod, Jefferson M. *An Index to English Language Newspapers Published in Korea, 1890–1940.* Seoul: National Assembly Library, 1965. 221 pp.

D. Yearbook

Korea Annual. 1964-- . Seoul: Hapdong Newsagency, 1964-- . Annual.

E. Chronology

Kai, Miwa and Philip B. Yampolsky. *Political Chronology of Japan, 1885--1957.* New York: East Asian Institute of Columbia University, 1957. 70 pp.

F. Historical Statistics

Japan Statistical Yearbook. Tokyo: Bureau of Statistics, Office of the Prime Minister, 1949-- . In Japanese and English.

Korea (Democratic People's Republic). Kukka Kyehoek Wiwonhoe. Chungang t'onggyeguk (Korea. State Planning Commission. Central Statistical Board). *Statistical Returns of National Economy of the Democratic People's Republic of Korea, 1946--1960.* Pyong-yang: Foreign Languages Publishing House, 1961. 189 pp.

XV. History of Oceania Including Australia and New Zealand

A. Encyclopedias and Handbook

Australian Encyclopaedia. Sidney: Angus & Robertson, 1958. 10 vols.

Encyclopaedia of New Zealand. A.H. McLintock, ed. Wellington: R.E. Owen, Govt. Printer, 1966. 3 vols.

Encyclopedia of the Philippines. 3d ed. Manila: E. Floro, 1950--1958. 20 vols.

Modern Encyclopaedia of Australia and New Zealand. Sydney: Melbourne: Horwitz-Grahame, 1964. 1199 pp.

Osborne, Charles, ed. *Australia, New Zealand and the South Pacific: A Handbook.* New York: Praeger, 1970. 580 pp.

B. Bibliographies

Allied Forces. *Annotated Bibliography of the Southwest Pacific and Adjacent Areas.* [n.p.] 1944--1945. 4 vols.

Blair, Emma H. and James A. Robertson. *The Philippine Islands, 1493-1898.* Cleveland,

OH: Arthur H. Clark, 1908. 55 vols. (Volume 53 is an annotated bibliography.)

Cammack, Floyd M. and Shiro Saito. *Pacific Island Bibliography.* New York: Scarecrow, 1962. 421 pp. (Supplements Taylor below.)

Crowley, Francis K. *South Australian History: A Survey for Research Students.* Adelaide: Libraries Board of South Australia, 1966. 200 pp.

Ferguson, John A. *Bibliography of Australia.* v. 1-- . Sydney; London: Angus & Robertson, 1941-- .

Hocken, Thomas M. *Bibliography of Literature Relating to New Zealand.* Wellington: Mackay, 1909. 619 pp. (Also Supplement, 1927.)

Taylor, C.R.H. *A Pacific Bibliography: Printed Matter Relating to the Native Peoples of Polynesia, Melanesia and Micronesia.* 2d ed. Oxford: Clarendon Press, 1965. 692 pp.

Wood, G.A. *A Guide for Students of New Zealand History.* Dunedin: University of Otago Press, 1973. 63 pp.

Writings in New Zealand History. Melbourne: University, 1940-- . (In *Historical Studies, Australia and New Zealand*, 1940-- . Annual.)

C. Biographical Source

Manuel, E. Arsenio. *Dictionary of Philippine Biography.* v. 1-- . Quezon City: Filipiniana, 1955-- . (In progress?)

XVI. Latin American and Caribbean History

A. Dictionaries, Encyclopedias and Handbooks

1. Historical

Martin, Michael and Gabriel Lovett, eds. *Encyclopedia of Latin American History.* Rev. ed., by L. Robert Hughes. Indianapolis, IN: Bobbs-Merrill, 1968. 348 pp.

The "Latin American Historical Dictionaries" series published by Scarecrow Press includes historical dictionaries on individual countries in Central and South America, e.g. Guatemala (rev. ed. 1973), Panama (1970), Puerto Rico and the U.S. Virgin Islands (1973).

2. General

Delpar, Helen. *Encyclopedia of Latin America*. New York: McGraw-Hill, 1974. 660 pp.

Véliz, Claudio. *Latin America and the Caribbean: A Handbook*. New York: Praeger, 1968. 840 pp.

B.   Bibliographies

Bayitch, Stojan A. *Latin America and the Caribbean: A Bibliographic Guide to Works in English*. Coral Gables, FL: University of Miami Press, 1967. 943 pp.

Chilcote, Ronald H. *Revolution and Structural Change in Latin America: A Bibliography on Ideology, Development, and the Radical Left (1930--1965)*. Stanford, CA: Hoover Institution on War, Revolution and Peace, 1970. 2 vols.

Dorn, Georgette M. *Latin America, Spain and Portugal: An Annotated Bibliography of Paperback Books*. 2d rev. ed. Washington, DC: Library of Congress, 1976. 328 pp.

Gerhard, Peter. *A Guide to the Historical Geography of New Spain*. New York: Cambridge Press, 1972. 476 pp.

Griffin, Charles C. *Latin America: A Guide to the Historical Literature*. Austin: University of Texas Press, 1971. 700 pp.

Handbook of Latin American Studies. 1935-- . Cambridge, MA: Harvard University Press, 1936--1947; Gainesville: University of Florida Press, 1948-- . Annual. (Currently: Alternate years are devoted to Humanities and to Social Sciences.)

Humphreys, R.A. *Latin American History: A Guide to the Literature in English*. London: Oxford University Press, 1958. 197 pp.

Pérez, Louis A., Jr. *The Cuban Revolutionary War, 1953--1958: A Bibliography*. Metu--chen, NJ: Scarecrow, 1976. 234 pp.

Ragatz, Lowell J. *A Guide for the Study of British Caribbean History, 1763--1834, Including the Abolition and Emancipation Movements*. Washington, DC: U.S. Government Printing Office, 1932. 725 pp.

Sable, Martin H. *A Guide to Latin American Studies*. Los Angeles: University of California, 1967. 2 vols.

Valdés, Nelson P. and Edwin Lieuwen. *The Cuban Revolution: A Research-Study Guide (1959--1969)*. Albuquerque: University of New Mexico Press, 1971. 230 pp.

Wilgus, Alva C. *Latin America in the Nineteenth Century: A Selected Bibliography of Books on Travel and Description Pub-*

lished in English. Metuchen, NJ: Scarecrow, 1973. 174 pp.

C.   Biographical Sources

Kay, Ernest. *Dictionary of Latin American and Caribbean Biography*. 2d ed. London: Melrose Press, 1971. 459 pp.

Who's Notable in Mexico. v. 1-- . Mexico, D.F.: Who's Who in Mexico, 1972-- .

Who's Who in Latin America. 3d ed. Stanford, CA: Stanford University Press, 1946--1951. 7 vols.

D.   Atlases

Condarco Morales, Ramiro. *Atlas Histórico de América*. La Paz: Ediciones Condarco, 1968. 185 pp.

Wilgus, Alva C. *Historical Atlas of Latin America: Political, Geographic, Economic, Cultural*. New and enlarged ed. New York: Cooper Square Publishers, 1967. 376 pp.

E.   Historical Statistics

Ruddle, Kenneth and Mukhtar Hamour, eds. *Statistical Abstract of Latin America*. 1955-- . Los Angeles: University of California at Los Angeles, Center of Latin American Studies, 1956-- . Irregular. (Also Supplements supplying statistics on particular topics and areas.)

XVII.   General History

A.   Encyclopedias, Handbooks, and Dictionaries

1.   Historical

Dupuy, R. Ernest and Trevor N. Dupuy. *The Encyclopedia of Military History; From 3500 B.C. to the Present*. Rev. ed. New York: Harper and Row, 1977. 1479 pp.

Eggenberger, David. *A Dictionary of Battles*. New York: Crowell, 1967. 536 pp.

Harbottle, Thomas B. *Dictionary of Battles*. Rev. ed. Revised by George Bruce. New York: Stein & Day, 1971. 333 pp.

2.   General

American University. Foreign Area Studies Division. *Area Handbooks*. Washington, DC: U.S. Government Printing Office, 1961-- .

Collier's Encyclopedia with Bibliography and Index. New York: Collier and Macmillan, 1976. 24 vols.

* *Encyclopedia Americana.* International edition. New York: The Americana Corp., 1972. 30 vols.

The Encyclopaedia Britannica. 11th ed. Cambridge: University Press, 1910--1911. 29 vols. Also: 2 supplement sets, 3 vols. (1922), 3 vols. (1926). Use also the 9th ed., Edinburgh: A.C. Black, 1875--1889, 25 vols.

The New Encyclopaedia Britannica. 15th ed. Chicago: Encyclopaedia Britannica, 1977. 30 vols.

Murray, James A.H. *A New English Dictionary on Historical Principles . . . .* Oxford: Clarendon Press, 1888--1928. 10 vols. in 13. (Also: Onions, Charles T. *The Shorter Oxford English Dictionary on Historical Principles.* 3d ed. Oxford: Clarendon Press, 1973. 2697 pp.)

B. Desk References

1. Style Manuals

A Manual of Style for Authors, Editors, and Copywriters. 12th ed. Chicago: University of Chicago, 1969. 559 pp.

Modern Language Association. *The MLA Style Sheet.* 2d ed. New York, 1970. 48 pp.

Turabian, Kate L. *A Manual for Writers of Term Papers, Theses, and Dissertations.* 4th ed. Chicago: University of Chicago Press, 1973. 224 pp.

2. Sources for Quotations

Bartlett, John. *Familiar Quotations: A Collection of Passages, Phrases and Proverbs Traced to Their Sources in Ancient and Modern Literature.* 14th ed. Boston: Little, Brown, 1968. 1768 pp.

Oxford Dictionary of English Proverbs. 3d ed. Oxford: Clarendon Press, 1970. 949 pp.

Palmer, Alan and Veronica Palmer. *Quotations in History: A Dictionary of Historical Quotations c.800 A.D. to the Present.* New York: Barnes and Noble, 1976. 354 pp.

Stevenson, Burton E. *The Home Book of Quotations, Classical and Modern.* 10th ed. New York: Dodd, Mead, 1967. 2858 pp.

3. Thesaurus

Roget, Peter M. *The Original Roget's Thesaurus of English Words and Phrases.* New ed. New York: St. Martin's, 1965 (c1962). 1485 pp.

C. Periodical Indexes

* *Bulletin of the Public Affairs Information Service (P.A.I.S.).* 1915-- . New York: Public Affairs Information Service, 1915-- . 44 times per year.

* *C.R.I.S., The Combined Retrospective Index Set to Journals in History, 1838--1974.* Arlington, VA: Carrollton Press, 1977-- .

Cumulated Magazine Subject Index, 1907--1949; A Cumulation of the F.W. Faxon Company's Annual Magazine Subject Index. Boston: G.K. Hall, 1964. 2 vols.

Guide to the American Historical Review, 1895--1945. Franklin D. Scott and Elaine Teigler, comps. Washington, DC: American Historical Assoc., 1945. (Found in the A.H.A. *Annual Report* for the year 1944, vol. 1, pt. 2, pp. 65--292.)

* *Historical Abstracts, 1450 to present: Bibliography of the World's Periodical Literature.* Santa Barbara, CA: ABC-Clio Press, 1955- . Originally covered the years 1775--1945, with vol. 17 (1971) expanded its coverage to years since 1945, and with vol. 19 (1973) expanded to cover the years 1450 to 1775.

* *Humanities Index.* v. 1-- , 1974-- . New York: H.W. Wilson, 1975-- . Quarterly. Formerly part of *Social Sciences & Humanities Index* (1966--1974), formerly *International Index* (1924--1965), formerly *Readers' Guide to Periodical Literature Supplement* (1916--1920).

* *Nineteenth Century Readers' Guide to Periodical Literature, 1890--1899.* New York: H.W. Wilson, 1944. 2 vols. (Also supplements, 1900--1922.)

* *Poole's Index to Periodical Literature.* Gloucester, MA: Peter Smith, 1882. 1 vol. (Supplements 1--5, Boston: Houghton Mifflin, 1893--1908. 5 vols.)

* *Readers' Guide to Periodical Literature.* 1900/1904-- . New York: H.W. Wilson, 1905-- . Semimonthly.

* *Social Sciences Citation Index*. 1973-- . Philadelphia, PA: Institute for Scientific Information, 1974-- . Three times per year.
* *Women Studies Abstracts*. v. 1, no. 1-- . Winter, 1972-- . Rush, NY: Rush Pub. Co., 1972-- . Quarterly.

D. Newspaper Indexes

Christian Science Monitor: Subject Index. v. 1-- . Boston, 1960-- .

* *New York Times Index*. 1851-- . New York: New York Times, 1913-- . (Earlier volumes have been reprinted by R.R. Bowker, New York.)

Palmer's Index to the Times Newspaper, 1790--June 1941. London: Palmer, 1868--1943.

Times, London. *Index to the Times*. 1906-- . London: Times, 1907-- . (Research Publications, Woodbridge, CT, have recently announced the republication of indexes to the *Times* newspaper for the years 1785-- .)

E. Essay Index

* *Essay and General Literature Index*. 1900/33-- . New York: H.W. Wilson, 1934-- .

F. Bibliographies

1. History Bibliographies

* American Historical Association. *Guide to Historical Literature*. Rev. ed. George F. Howe et al., eds. New York: Macmillan, 1961. 997 pp.

American Universities Field Staff. *A Select Bibliography: Asia, Africa, Eastern Europe, Latin America*. New York: American Universities Field Staff, 1960. 534 pp. Plus Supplements.

The Foreign Affairs 50--Year Bibliography: New Evaluations of Significant Books on International Relations 1920--1970. New York: Bowker, 1972. 964 pp. A consolidation, condensation and revision of previous, separate volumes.

Hunt, Robert N.C. *Books on Communism: A Bibliography*. London: Ampersand, 1959. 333 pp.

International Bibliography of Historical Sciences. 1926-- . New York: H.W. Wilson, 1930-- .

Kuehl, Warren F. *Dissertations in History; An Index to Dissertations Completed in History Departments of United States and Canadian Universities,* *1873--1960*. Lexington, KY: University of Kentucky Press, 1965. 249 pp. (Also: *1961--June 1970*. 1972. 237 pp.)

McGarry, Daniel D. and Sarah White, ed. *World Historical Fiction Guide*. 2d ed. Metuchen, NJ: Scarecrow Press, 1973. 629 pp.

Milden, James Wallace. *The Family in Past Time; A Guide to the Literature*. New York: Garland, 1977. 200 pp.

Particular journals such as *Middle East Journal, American Historical Review, American Quarterly* and *Journal of Modern History*, to name a few, carry, or did carry, reviews of books/lists of articles and books in their respective fields.

2. Bibliographies of Bibliographies that include History

* *American Reference Books Annual*. 1970-- . Littleton, CO: Libraries Unlimited, 1970-- .

Besterman, Theodore. *A World Bibliography of Bibliographies*. 4th ed. Totowa, NJ: Rowman and Littlefield, 1965--66. 5 vols.

* *Bibliographic Index: A Cumulative Bibliography of Bibliographies*. 1937/42-- . New York: H.W. Wilson, 1945-- .

* *Library of Congress Catalog -- Books: Subjects; a Cumulative List of Works Represented by Library of Congress Printed Cards, 1950 to Present*. Washington, DC: Library of Congress, 1955-- .

* Sheehy, Eugene P. *A Guide to Reference Books*. 9th ed. Chicago: American Library Association, 1976. 1033 pp.

Walford, Albert J. *Guide to Reference Material*. 3d ed. London: Library Association, 1973--77. 3 vols.

* White, Carl M. *Sources of Information in the Social Sciences*. 2d ed. Chicago: American Library Association, 1973. 720 pp.

G. Book Review Sources

* *Book Review Digest*. 1905-- . New York: H.W. Wilson, 1905-- . Monthly.

* *Book Review Index*. v. 1-- . Detroit, MI: Gale Research, 1965-- . Bimonthly.

Brewster, John W. and Joseph A. McLeod. *Index to Book Reviews in Historical*

Periodicals. 1972-- . Metuchen, NJ: Scarecrow Press, 1975-- . Irregular.

* *Current Book Review Citations.* v. 1-- , 1976-- . New York: H.W. Wilson, 1976-- . Monthly.

* *Humanities Index.* v. 1-- , 1974-- . New York: H.W. Wilson, 1975-- . Quarterly.

* *An Index to Book Reviews in the Humanities.* v. 1-- . Williamston, MI: Phillip Thomson, 1960-- . Annual.

* *Social Sciences Citation Index.* 1973-- . Philadelphia: Institute for Scientific Information, 1974-- . Three times per year.

H. Biographical Sources

1. Bibliography of Biographies

* *Biography Index: A Cumulative Index to Biographical Material in Books and Magazines.* 1946-- . New York: H.W. Wilson, 1949. Quarterly.

Hyamson, Albert M. *A Dictionary of Universal Biography of all Ages and of all Peoples.* 2d ed. London: Routledge and Kegan Paul, 1951. 679 pp.

2. Biographies

* *Contemporary Authors: A Bio-Bibliographical Guide to Current Authors and Their Works.* v. 1-- . Detroit: Gale, 1962-- . Irregular.

* *Current Biography: Who's News and Why.* v. 1-- . New York: H.W. Wilson, 1940-- . Monthly.

International Who's Who. 1935-- . London: Europa, 1935-- . Annual.

Ireland, Norma O. *Index to Women of the World from Ancient to Modern Times.* Westwood, MA: Faxon, 1970. 573 pp.

The McGraw-Hill Encyclopedia of World Biography. New York: McGraw-Hill, 1973. 12 vols.

New Century Cyclopedia of Names, ed. by Clarence L. Barnhart. New York: Appleton, 1954. 3 vols.

New York Times Obituaries Index. 1858-- 1968. New York: New York Times, 1970. 1136 pp.

Webster's Biographical Dictionary. Springfield, MA: Merriam, 1972. 1697 pp.

I. Atlases and Gazetteers

1. Historical

Atlas of Discovery. Text by Gail Roberts. New York: Crown, 1973. 192 pp.

Atlas zur Weltgeschichte: Vorzeit, Altertum, Mittelalter, Neuzeit. Braunschweig: Westermann, 1956. 3 vols.

Banks, Arthur. *A World Atlas of Military History.* v. 1-- . New York: Hippocrene Books, 1973-- .

Gilbert, Martin. *Recent History Atlas: 1870 to the Present Day.* 1st American ed. New York: Macmillan, 1966. 130 pp.

Kinder, Hermann and Werner Hilgemann. *The Anchor Atlas of World History: From the Stone Age to the Eve of the French Revolution.* Garden City, NY: Anchor/Doubleday, 1975. 299 pp.

Meer, Frederic van der. *Atlas of Western Civilization.* English version. 2d rev. ed. Princeton, NJ: Van Nostrand, 1960. 240 pp.

Muir's Historical Atlas: Ancient, Medieval and Modern. New York: Barnes and Noble, 1963. 116 pp.

Palmer, Robert R. *Atlas of World History.* Chicago: Rand, McNally, 1957. 216 pp.

Palmer, Robert R. *Historical Atlas of the World.* Chicago: Rand, McNally. 40 pp.

Sellman, Roger R. *An Outline Atlas of World History.* New York: St. Martin's Press, 1970. 127 pp.

Shepherd, William R., ed. *Shepherd's Historical Atlas.* 9th ed. New York: Barnes & Noble, 1973. 127 pp.

2. General

The Columbia Lippincott Gazetteer of the World. Leon E. Seltzer, ed. New York: Columbia University Press; Philadelphia: J.B. Lippincott, Co., 1962. 2148 pp.

The Earth and Man: A Rand McNally World Atlas. New York: Rand McNally, 1972. 439 pp.

Hammond Contemporary World Atlas. New Census ed. Garden City, NY: Doubleday, 1974. 256 pp.

The Times Atlas of the World: Comprehensive Edition. 5th ed. London: Times Books, 1975. 263 pp.

Webster's Geographical Dictionary. Rev. ed. Springfield, MA: G. & C. Merriam Co., 1969. 1324 pp.

J. Yearbooks

The Annual Register of World Events. v. 1-- , 1758-- . New York: St. Martin's Press, 1761-- .

Statesman's Yearbook. 1864-- . New York: Macmillan, 1864-- .

K. Chronologies

Bond, John James. *Handy-book of Rules and Tables for Verifying Dates with the Christian Era.* London: Bell, 1875. 465 pp.

Butler, Audrey. *Everyman's Dictionary of Dates.* 6th ed. New York: Dutton, 1971. 518 pp.

Damon, Charles Ripley. *The American Dictionary of Dates, 458--1920.* Morristown, TN: The Globe Book Co., 1921. 3 vols. (Includes texts of a few documents.)

Freeman-Grenville, Greville S.P. *Chronology of World History: A Calendar of Principal Events from 3000 B.C. to A.D. 1973.* Totowa, NJ: Rowman & Littlefield, 1975. 753 pp.

Grun, Bernard. *The Timetables of History: A Horizontal Linkage of People and Events.* New York: Simon and Schuster, 1975. 661 pp.

Langer, William L. *An Encyclopedia of World History: Ancient, Medieval, and Modern Chronologically Arranged.* 5th ed. Boston: Houghton Mifflin, 1972. 1569 pp.

Steinberg, Sigfrid H. *Historical Tables, 58 B.C.--A.D. 1972.* 9th ed. New York: St. Martin's, 1973. 269 pp.

A series of chronology-fact books of various groups has been published by Oceana, Dobbs Ferry, NY. Among those published to date are:

The Germans in America 1607--1970 (1973)

The Chinese in America 1820--1973 (1973)

The Puerto Ricans (1973)

Similar chronology and fact books have been published by Oceana for England (1974), Ireland (1973) and a dozen other countries. Aimed primarily at the high-school age-group, these are elementary for the undergraduate, but useful.

L. Statistics

Demographic Yearbook: Annuaire Démographique. 1948-- . New York: United Nations, Statistical Office, 1949-- .

Statistical Yearbook: Annuaire Statistique. 1948-- . New York: United Nations, Statistical Office. 1949-- . (Preceded by *Statistical Yearbook of the League of Nations,* 1926--1942/44.)

The World Almanac and Book of Facts. 1868-- . New York: Newspaper Enterprise Assoc., 1868-- . (Annual)

M. Government Documents

Guide to League of Nations Publications: A Bibliographical Survey of the Work of the League, 1920--1947. Hans Aufricht, comp. New York: Columbia University Press, 1951. 701 pp.

International Bibliography, Information, Documentation: IBID. v. 1-- . New York: Bowker/Unipub, 1973-- . (Covers allied independent agencies as well as the U.N.)

UNDEX: United Nations Documents Index. v. 1-- . New York: United Nations, 1970-- . Published in 3 series: Series A, Subject Index; Series B, Country Index; Series C, List of Documents Issued. (Supersedes *United Nations Documents Index, UNDI,* 1950--1973.)

N. Documents Collection

Viorst, Milton, ed. *Great Documents of Western Civilization.* Radnor, PA: Chilton, 1965. 388 pp.

XVIII. Union Lists of Holdings: Books, Newspapers, Microfilms, Manuscripts, etc.

African Newspapers in Selected American Libraries. 3d ed. Washington, DC: Library of Congress, 1965. 135 pp.

Boehm, Eric and Lalit Adolphus. *Historical Periodicals: An Annotated List of Historical and Related Serial Publications.* Santa Barbara, CA: Clio Press, 1961. 618 pp.

Caron, Pierre and Marc Jaryc. *World List of Historical Periodicals.* New York: H.W. Wilson Co., 1939. 391 pp.

Charno, Steven M., ed. *Latin American Newspapers in United States Libraries.* Austin: University of Texas Press, 1969. 633 pp.

Faye, Helen. *Picture Sources: An Introductory List.* New York: Special Libraries Association, 1959. 115 pp.

Gerould, Winifred Gregory, ed. *American Newspapers, 1821--1936: A Union List of Files Available in the United States and Canada.* New York: H.W. Wilson, 1937. 807 pp.

Hale, Richard Walden, Jr., ed. *Guide to Photocopied Historical Materials in the United States and Canada*. Ithaca, NY: Cornell University Press for the American Historical Association, 1961. 241 pp.

* *Library of Congress Catalog -- Books: Subjects, 1950--1954*. Ann Arbor, MI: Edwards, 1955. 20 vols. (Also 22 vols. for 1955--1959, 25 vols. for 1960--1964, 42 vols. for 1965--1969, and 100 vols. for 1970--1974.)

* *National Union Catalog: A Cumulative Author List*. 1956-- . Washington, DC: Library of Congress, 1958-- . Preceded by: U.S. Library of Congress. *A Catalog of Books Represented by the Library of Congress Printed Cards, Issued to July 1942*. Ann Arbor: Edwards, 1942--1946. 167 vols. Supplemented by later cumulations.

New Serial Titles: A Union List of Serials Commencing Publication After December 31, 1949. Washington, DC: Library of Congress, 1953-- .

Philadelphia Bibliographical Center and Union Library Catalogue. *Union List of Microfilms*. Cumulation 1949--1959. Eleanor E. Campion, ed. Ann Arbor: J.W. Edwards, 1961. 2 vols.

Union Catalogue of Asian Publications, 1965--1970. David E. Hall, ed. London: Mansell, 1971. 4 vols. (Also annual Supplements, published since 1973.)

U.S. Library of Congress. *The National Union Catalog of Manuscript Collections*. 1959/61-- . Hamden, CT: Shoe String, 1962-- .

* *Union List of Serials in Libraries of the United States and Canada*, ed. by Edna Brown Titus. 3d ed. New York: Wilson, 1965. 5 vols.

U.S. Library of Congress. Catalog Publication Division. *Newspapers in Microform: Foreign Countries, 1848--1972*. Washington, DC, 1973. 269 pp.

U.S. Library of Congress. Catalog Publication Division. *Newspapers in Microform: United States 1948--72*. Washington, DC, 1973. 1056 pp.

XIX. Guides to Other Collections

Ash, Lee. *Subject Collections: A Guide to Special Book Collections and Subject Emphases as Reported by University, College, Public, and Special Libraries and Museums in the United States and Canada*. 5th ed. New York: Bowker, 1978. 1184 pp.

Bartley, Russell H. and Stuart L. Wagner. *Latin America in Basic Historical Collections: A Working Guide*. Stanford, CA: Hoover Institution Press, 1972. 217 pp.

Collison, Robert L. *Directory of Libraries and Special Collections on Asia and North Africa*. Hamden, CT: Archon Books, 1970. 123 pp.

Columbia University. Oral History Research Office. *The Oral History Collection of Columbia University*. 3d ed. Elizabeth B. Mason and Louis M. Starr, eds. New York, 1973. 477 pp.

Directory of Historical Societies and Agencies in the United States and Canada, compiled and edited by Donna McDonald. 11th ed. Nashville, TN: American Association for State and Local History, 1978. 474 pp.

Grimsted, Patricia K. *Archives and Manuscript Repositories in the USSR: Moscow and Leningrad*. Princeton, NJ: Princeton University Press, 1972. 436 pp.

Hamer, Philip M. *A Guide to Archives and Manuscripts in the United States*. New Haven, CT: Yale University Press for the National Historical Publications Committee, 1961. 775 pp.

Haro, Robert P. *Latin Americana Research in the United States: A Guide and Directory*. Chicago: American Library Association, 1971. 111 pp.

Jackson, William V. *Library Guide for Brazilian Studies*. Pittsburgh, PA: University of Pittsburgh Book Centers, 1964. 197 pp.

Meckler, Alan M. and Ruth McMullin. *Oral History Collections*. New York: R.R. Bowker, 1975. 344 pp.

The National Register of Historic Places 1976. Washington, DC: U.S. Government Printing Office, 1976. 978 pp.

Shumway, Gary L. *Oral History in the United States: A Directory*. New York: Oral History Assoc., 1971. 120 pp.

Simmons, Johns S.G. *Russian Bibliography, Libraries and Archives*. Twickenham, Eng.: Anthony C. Hall, 1973. 94 pp.

Vanderbilt, Paul. *Guide to the Special Collections of Prints and Photographs in the Library of Congress*. Washington, DC: U.S. Government Printing Office, 1955. 200 pp.

XX. Guides to the Reference Sources

Barzun, Jacques and Henry F. Graff. *The Modern Researcher*. 3d ed. New York: Harcourt Brace Jovanovich, 1977. 397 pp.

Benjamin, Jules R. *A Student's Guide to History*. New York: St. Martin's Press, 1975. 122 pp.

Galbraith, Vivian H. *Introduction to the Use of the Public Records*. Oxford: Oxford University Press, 1952. 112 pp.

* Gray, Wood et al. *Historian's Handbook: A Key to the Study and Writing of History*. 2d ed. Boston: Houghton Mifflin, 1964. 95 pp.

* McCoy, F.N. *Researching and Writing in History: A Practical Handbook for Students*. Berkeley: University of California Press, 1974. 100 pp.

Morley, Charles. *Guide to Research in Russian*

History. Syracuse, NY: Syracuse University Press, 1951. 227 pp.

* Poulton, Helen J. *The Historian's Handbook: A Descriptive Guide to Reference Works*. Norman, OK: University of Oklahoma Press, 1972. 304 pp.

XXI. Vocational Guidance for Students of History

American Historical Association. Institutional Services Program. *Careers for Students of History*, ed. by Sally Gregory Kohlstedt. Washington, DC, 1977. 70 pp.

Guidelines for Proceeding

The questions below are designed to lead a student through a library search on a term paper topic in history. Some questions will lead to valuable materials: others will lead to dead ends. The questions pretty much follow the chapters in this book, so if any questions need clarification, refer to the appropriate chapter.

1. Choose my topic (Chapter 1).

2. Prepare bibliography cards (Chapter 1).

3. Narrow my topic (Chapter 2):
   a. What encyclopedias and bibliographies listed in Appendix 3 are most useful?
   b. Do the subject headings in the card catalog help me?
   c. Do the terms used in the table of contents or the indexes of any books suggest ways to narrow the topic?

4. What books can I find (Chapter 3)?
   a. What bibliographies of bibliographies does the reference librarian suggest?
   b. What other bibliographies can I locate through Appendix 3?

5. Which of these books does my library have (Chapter 4)?
   a. What subject heading(s) in the subject heading book most precisely describe my topic?
   b. What related headings are suggested by "sa" and "xx" in the subject heading book and by "see also" references in the card catalog?
   c. When I check the above headings in the card catalog, what books appear most useful?

6. What essays are there on my topic (Chapter 5)?
   a. Are there pertinent, brief passages in other books shelved close to those books I found?
   b. Does the *Essay and General Literature Index* list short chapters on my topic?

7. Evaluating books (Chapter 6).
   a. On what books am I primarily basing my paper?
   b. Have these books appeared in good, selective bibliographies?
   c. Have they been reviewed favorably? Unfavorably? Why? (Check the book review sources listed in Appendix 3.)
   d. Have I checked the standard biographical sources to discover what is the reputation of my authors? What other work they have done?
   e. What do I think of each book in comparison with others?

8. Collecting current information. This is especially important for topics of recent controversy (Chapter 7).
   a. Have I looked at general indexes like *Humanities Index*? (Check Appendix 3.)
   b. Have I looked at comprehensive historical indexes? (Check Appendix 3.)
   c. Have I looked at historical abstracting services? (Check Appendix 3.)
   d. Have I found any newspaper indexes that might help? (Check Appendix 3.)

9. Will government documents help me? If so, I should use the indexes listed in Appendix 3 and ask a reference librarian for guidance.

10. Do I need some biographical material?
    a. Is the person alive? Dead?
    b. What nationality is the person?
    c. Knowing *a* and *b* above, which biographical sources listed in Appendix 3 will be most useful?

11. Using other libraries (Chapter 11).
    a. If important books and articles are not in my library, do I have time to request interlibrary loans or photocopies?
    b. Shall I visit another library?

Index of Titles

Notes

Notes

Notes

Notes

Notes